Organizing and Big Scary Goals

Organizing and Big Scary Goals

Working With Discomfort and Doubt To Create Real Life Order

Sara S. Skillen

Columbus, Ohio

Unless otherwise noted, all photographs ©Mary Rice, 2019.

Organizing and Big Scary Goals: Working With Discomfort and Doubt To Create Real Life Order

Published by Gatekeeper Press
2167 Stringtown Rd, Suite 109
Columbus, OH 43123-2989
www.GatekeeperPress.com

Copyright © 2019 by Sara S. Skillen
All rights reserved. Neither this book, nor any parts within it may be sold or reproduced in any form or by any electronic or mechanical means, including information storage and retrieval systems without permission in writing from the author. The only exception is by a reviewer, who may quote short excerpts in a review.

ISBN (paperback): 9781642378177
eISBN: 9781642378184

Contents

Foreword vii
Introduction xiii

Chapter 1 Organized Shame – And a Deal 1
Chapter 2 Surrounded by Stuff, Nerves, and More Shame 19
Chapter 3 We All Fall Down 33
Chapter 4 Who's Judging Who? 47
Chapter 5 I Think I'm Getting It, But . . . 63
Chapter 6 A Long, Slow Break 73
Chapter 7 Back in the Saddle 85
Chapter 8 Experimentation 97
Chapter 9 The One "How-To" Chapter 107
Chapter 10 It's Still Big and Still Scary 125
Chapter 11 The Rest of the Story 137

Acknowledgements 151
References 155

To Guy

Foreword

I often joke that books on organizing make me want to throw up. With all due respect to their authors, most were not written for my tribe—adults with ADHD. If you browsed my bookshelf, you would find a bookmark in all my how-to-organize books, showing where I gave up and stopped reading. No doubt, those books are popular and helpful to the general population, and I admit to getting one good idea from each of them. But I discontinued reading once boredom surpassed my interest. Despite good common-sense tips for people with good common sense, most of those books discouraged me. The most informed and inspirational authors who don't understand me don't inspire me.

Like most people with ADHD, I'm organizationally challenged. My neurological difference is invisible to most people, but the effects of it can embarrass me. Organized individuals who try to help, despite their generous efforts and best intentions, sometimes offend me. My organizational challenges are not due to apathy, lack of intelligence, or laziness. But the effects of my brain difference can be immobilizing, especially when disorganization is obstructing me from meeting my needs at a critical time.

For months after moving to Los Angeles from Nashville as a young adult, the only people I knew were my co-workers, and most of them lived far from me. About all I did those first lonely months was drive from Santa Monica to Van Nuys each morning, work alone in a small windowless office, and return home to my tiny apartment overlooking an alley. I stopped walking to the beach on weekends because watching couples enjoying their lives made me lonelier. Before realizing I was depressed, I opened my eyes one morning to a bedroom that looked like a tornado-ravaged trailer. A partially skimmed paperback, *How to Get Control of Your Time and Your Life*, had taken up residence on my unmade bed. Trying to slog through that book only amplified my depression. I was becoming a self-loathing slob. I lacked motivation to do anything the author recommended. Not only was I alienated from my neighbors and a lovely community, I was neglecting my nest and daily tasks that should have been manageable. I survived that dark period by taking a class at UCLA, where I made a few friends, and by throwing that book away. I became a good-enough housekeeper to entertain new friends occasionally and recovered my normally bright mood and positive outlook.

Sara Skillen's book is different from other organizing books in important ways. Self-disclosure about her "big scary goal" gives her a credible voice for people wired like me. I had never framed my aversion to organizing as being fear-based until I read this book. Men are not supposed to be afraid, of course. And we deny denial…I just didn't have time, energy, or interest in being tidy.

The thought of organizing and filing papers has always overwhelmed me, and I haven't wanted to confront it. To be honest, I still don't want to, but I have learned that I can, thanks to Sara Skillen. Sara has compassion for individuals who are neurologically atypical, anxiously avoidant, or hopelessly resigned. She presents alternatives to our aversion to confronting inherent challenges in prioritizing, activating, and sustaining effort, all of which are central features of attention disorders. We don't have to give up and pretend we don't care. We don't have to save face by denying that we lack organizational competence. There is no reason for embarrassment when you can embrace your fear and start where you are.

Before Sara let me see her manuscript, I didn't believe anyone could write a book on organizing that I would want to read all the way to the end. And she was ambivalent about whether readers would identify with her own "big scary goal." Revealing her private fear must have been uncomfortable. Before confronting it, she perceived the object of her fear as an embarrassing weakness. I found her disclosure refreshing. Her willingness to experience discomfort in telling on herself made me comfortable. Sara is as disarmingly human and credible in her writing as she is with her clients. Relatable snippets of her evolving story, inserted throughout this book, grabbed and held my interest and my fragile attention.

Unlike other books on organizing, this book addresses the emotional challenge right from the start, demonstrating the author's patience and compassion for how organizationally challenged people feel. Beyond the entertaining and pertinent personal stories, Sara offers a manageable path for tackling tasks that her readers would rather avoid.

Sara's skillful way of demystifying organizing is inspiring. While you may still experience some fear and aversion, this book will inspire you to try on a new perspective, new strategies and new tools. Your willingness to transcend uncomfortable feelings will help you activate and keep your wheels on the tracks.

Sara believes there is not one best way for everyone to organize their environment and their daily tasks, and I'm grateful for that. She embraces "good enough" as a way to move beyond resistance and negativity that often come with having tried to live up to others' expectations. She aims to clarify and simplify the process so her readers and clients can move beyond their fears, develop their own style, and achieve their goals.

Learning how to manage time and workspace efficiently with creative strategies and new tools is inherently rewarding. An even bigger reward is attaining your most important personal goals.

This book is not just for people like me who have an attention disorder. It can help anyone to overcome immobilizing perfectionism, hopeless resignation, and fear that may arise when confronting challenges associated with organizing. Sara Skillen has taken what I once believed was too overwhelming and complex to manage, and made it manageable. Her compassion, vision, and resourcefulness make this book worth reading.

Terry M. Huff, LCSW
Author of *Living Well with ADHD*

Introduction

Get organized. How does that phrase land for you? Does it conjure ease? Anxiety? Confidence? Disgust? Comfort? Bewilderment? When I wanted to start a business roughly eight years ago, I typed "what can you do if you're organized" into the search bar in my browser—and now here I am. It's a cliché in my world, because for me, organization is a critical, supportive, and regulating life skill that most of us cannot function without, especially in the twenty-first century. It's like brushing your teeth or tying your shoes. Unless you live in an entirely energy-efficient, minimalist, self-sustaining house off the grid with no need for a regular job and plenty of household help (and lucky you, if you do), you need some facility with organizing, time management, and task-management skills to navigate life. Aside from the basics, being organized and productive can play a role in calming and healing so many issues—shame, discomfort, isolation, stress, and loss of income, to name a few.

As I'm writing this introduction, I'm seeing a text come through from a client—it's a message with pictures of their progress. They are gaining momentum, and I'm gratified when my work allows clients to find some peace, to feel relief, and to smooth some of the rough edges of a life that previously seemed totally unmanageable. Whether it's getting a desk drawer sorted and categorized or unloading twenty years' worth of untouched holiday decor from the attic, the process of successful stuff management lifts the spirit and calms the soul. It's never only about the stuff—but the stuff behind the stuff.

When I finally did become a professional organizer, it was always in my heart that encouraging people to find their own way to that sort of healing was my mission. I didn't call it healing at first, but I've come to embrace the idea now. We may kid ourselves into thinking we can block out the clutter and chaos, but anyone who has stepped into a serene, comfortable, intentionally-organized space knows that there is an immediate effect on the psyche. Anyone who can look at their calendar or a task list and know that they are on top of things feels in control, so much so that they often take it for granted. I think these feelings are why, every few years or so, the topic is bolstered by some sort of craze that gets people revved up to "get organized." We all yearn to feel comfortable with our space and time, but many of my clients lose their way with organization and have challenges finding what fits. The organizing technique *du jour* doesn't necessarily work for them. They struggle.

Yet everyone has something they struggle to accomplish, implement, or maintain—that big, elusive, and sometimes secreted thing you feel you aren't very good at. I certainly have things I'm not good at, and I set out to explore what shifts might occur if I worked to be better at something that challenges and even scares me. This book quickly became a part of that process, because empathy, understanding, and the ability to relate to my clients on some level is a high priority for me. I always want to walk my talk and do my best to speak with authenticity.

I resisted writing any sort of organizing or productivity book for a long time because I felt that what needed to be said already had been—in many other ways by many wiser people. It's not lost on me that books on organizing or productivity often do not resonate with those who wrestle with crowded closets and too many commitments. I also thought perhaps I needed some sort of clever hook to get my point across, and I am very aware that lots of the ideas I use in working with clients are not my own, but re-characterizations of things I've read or learned about in other settings, as well as my personal past experience. Most of us who organize professionally are playing variations on the same theme, which is a great thing because our unique ways of presenting universal concepts give people options to choose from. But I also noticed from the beginning of my organizing career that clients sometimes came up with their own ideas and strategies that surpassed whatever I might have suggested, and I learned from those experiences.

So why a book now? I've always loved to write, and my blog has often given me an outlet for pondering and working through my strategies and ideas to help others. Some of the ideas presented here grew out of the blog and the various comments and responses I received. Many thoughts came through intuition, and still others from observation and listening. The ideas seemed to lead to questions, then to answers, and then back to questions again, so I started recording them.

As I continue supporting clients in untangling their organizing and productivity knots, some of the broader questions that continually resurface are:

- Where, and how, should you begin something that doesn't come naturally or easily—whether it's clearing a closet, managing a calendar, running a business, or mastering any new, challenging skill? How do you stare down and face a Big Scary Goal?
- If you do develop competence and master the Big Scary Goal, how can you keep from falling off the figurative bike and back into old habits?
- When chaos hits (as it inevitably does), and you do fall off the bike (which you will), how do you get back on without feeling like a failure? Without saying "to hell with it" and giving up?
- Ultimately, how do you "flip the switch" with organizing habits? How do you maintain the balance to develop a sustainable pattern?

For some people, a mixture of ongoing confusion, boredom, and frustration sets in once they begin work on their Big Scary Goals. The organizing-specific questions, tension, lack of confidence, and doubts swirl: Is it possible to still be organized even if you don't let go of much stuff? What should you keep? And why? And where should you store it? And why didn't the file system or the app or the plastic bins you purchased work? Why does merely processing the mail every day seem so unattainable? Are you doing this organizing stuff right?

That last one is a biggie. There's a subliminal mental panic button that gets pushed with the driving desire to do everything the "right way." Perfectionism is a best friend of procrastination. Then there's also shame—shame that stands right in front of the Big Scary Goal, the goal that seems easy for everyone except you. What is the right amount of being organized? How can organization fit into an everyday, overwhelmed, distracted life—especially when shame and uncertainty take hold?

To start thinking about the answers to all of these questions, we might begin with balance.

Balanced organization is the state of equilibrium in which there are neither too many nor too few items or tasks for the user(s) of a space to maintain; feeling contented, effective, and reasonably in control of one's surroundings—the Goldilocks zone of organization.

Sometimes people think I must organize all the time—as if I spend most waking moments concerned with decluttering, sorting, labeling, containerizing, arranging, color-coding, and so on. But that's not what organization is supposed to do for me. I hate to burst the bubble, but it's not a hobby. For me, organization is a baseline activity that allows me to live sanely and to weather conflict and stress more gracefully. I do what I need to do to more or less maintain that level of sanity, and teach others to do the same. Living with calm in our environment is clearly preferable for most of us, as is living healthy, living out dreams, and living responsibly. But at the same time that many of my clients strive for balanced organization, they are bombarded with external messages that tell them they aren't doing it right, doing it aesthetically, or doing it in sync with others' expectations. I don't care for those sorts of messages, but I hope to take a closer look at some of them and help you think about how you might respond when you receive them.

While looking at these messages, I'm going to take a look at a parallel goal of my own that I hope will put me in a position to better understand and demonstrate how to attack an intimidating challenge. My own personal journey to overcome and meet my Big Scary Goal is also outlined on the following pages because I needed to put myself in an uncomfortable, and *unthinkable*, spot in order to see how I could dig my way out. I learned unexpected things along the way, and I think these things are worth connecting to how people might feel about improving their organization skills, or mastering any elusive ability for that matter. My Big Scary Goal also tracked pretty nicely with the idea of balance.

If you scan through the book, you'll see individual stories. The people featured are fictional, but with tidbits shaped from my own experiences—no one described is an actual client or based upon anyone I know. The stories illustrate all sorts of organizing challenges, and most of them end before any kind of clear-cut resolution to their problem takes place. I'm hoping that you will take note of the journey as opposed to the destination, at least at first. You'll have an opportunity, if you like, to imagine your own ideas for one story's ending. I'll be even more excited if I learn that some of you write or create a conclusion to your own story.

In each chapter, you'll also find "The Subplot," a nonfiction account of my journey through and to my uncomfortable goal. My information is primarily anecdotal—no research or statistics or comparisons. I needed to write what I have experienced and seen, heard, and felt. I do have one "how-to" section in Chapter 9, but otherwise, the stories should resonate in a way that allows you to reflect on your own unique progress. At the end of each chapter is a section I've dubbed a "Scribble," a few questions that may be used for further exploration. You can jot down answers or even sketch out ideas using the space provided.

For simplicity, when I use the term "organizing," I mean for it to encompass anything that requires planning, decision-making, arrangement, or the creation of logical systems. Time management is organizing time. Task management is organizing tasks. Organizing and productivity do not exist happily without each other. I like to work with, and write about, both.

I believe you can discover ways to dig yourself out of difficulty—literally and figuratively. The question is whether you will dig with tension and fear, or with relaxation and patience. Think about what resources you can call upon to help you dig, because none of us really does it alone. The world is full of stories of inspiring people who have conquered unusual challenges. There are fantastic characteristics, strengths, and capabilities within that many of us never manage to scratch the surface of. What if you took some time to pull your hidden capabilities up from the depths? What if you learned how you could put your own unique stamp on them? Are we still talking about just getting organized?

What follows is not a "how-to" book, but rather a "how-might-you?" book. How might you approach improved organization or better time management with a more relaxed way to explore what works best for you? I hope that the words that follow will be a starting point for you. I hope that you're empowered to develop your own distinctive style of working through paper piles, overflowing inboxes, or closets. I hope you develop comfort with a process that is initially awkward, doubt-ridden, and frustrating, but ultimately rewarding. There are so many ways to move forward.

Shall we begin our search for some balance together?

CHAPTER 1

Organized Shame - And a Deal

Shame (noun):

1. the painful feeling arising from the consciousness of something dishonorable, improper, ridiculous, etc., done by oneself or another.

(S)he was overcome with shame.

—www.dictionary.com

The scene: You bought a glossy home-lifestyle magazine on impulse in the grocery checkout, after you were exhausted from shopping with your three kids, and when the wily store marketing gods knew you would be weak, distracted, and ready to make a purchase you didn't actually need. You couldn't wait to get home, relax, and check out all of the snazzy ideas. You'd seen organizing TV shows, too, and you believed you were finally ready to get your home and life into beautiful, ordered, color-coded shape.

Upon arriving at that home, you skipped getting those canned goods and boxes put away so you could curl up on the couch with the magazine. "Get Organized!" the cover gleefully shouted, as if organization was something you could simply walk out the door to purchase and hang onto indefinitely.

As you flipped the pages trying to tune out the sounds of the TV, your twins arguing, and an excessive amount of water running *somewhere* in the house, you sighed over the fabulously styled pantry, the perfectly labeled, matching baskets in the bedroom closet, the books on a shelf arranged by color and height. The home-office page had an immaculate, sleek desk with a healthy potted plant, two artfully placed notebooks, and a fountain pen next to the laptop. There were no scattered Legos, no piles of school paperwork, and no extension cords in sight. Maybe if you just went out and bought some of those canvas bins, a label maker, or the matching hangers, everything would fall into place.

It would totally look like this, right?

©belchonok, 123RF.com

Cue the angel chorus. It would be amazing, magical, and your life would finally be different. When you completed all of your rooms and managed to get your closets to look the exact same way you could post all about it—maybe even get one of those magazines to come take pictures and feature your family! Satisfied that you knew what you were going to do next, you made a plan to buy some of the stuff the magazine recommended—see how that worked there? Whew, time for a nap! The scene fades to soothing music . . . and . . . cut.

But wait—let's think about this for a moment. Will you consistently buy all of the same brands of canned goods, in the same size, so that they line up neatly every time? Will you always take the time to pour cereals and pastas out of their boxes into pretty, clear, cleverly labeled containers? Do you wear clothing that is more or less all solid colors and similar styles, with no outliers, like a formal dress or an ugly Christmas sweater? How about your electronics and appliances—do they miraculously function without cords? Are you going to install lighting in your kitchen, master closet, or garage so that everything pops when you gaze lovingly at it?

Or do you, like most people (including me) buy what's needed at the time, or what you like, or what makes you feel good in the moment? Do you receive gifts or family heirlooms that don't exactly match what you already own? Do you have a hobby that seems to encourage accumulation? Have you lost weight, gained it, lost it again, and kept all the clothing from all three phases? Do you hate opening mail and dealing with the junk? Have you been dealing with grief and not up for purging and sorting? How does all of that stuff fit together into what we are told "organized" should look like?

When organizing became a popular topic in the media, along came the stylized photographs all over blogs, boards, and social media sites—pictures that remind me of the heavily edited bodies or faces on fashion models that most of us cannot ever hope to emulate. The perfection of these photos is, of course, carefully calculated to help us want what we don't have—so that we will be willing to pay for some version of it. Most of us recognize it intellectually, but our hearts still yearn for the uniformity of the clear countertops and matching file folders. Even I get caught up in organizing envy, wondering if I should redo my bookshelves or my perfectly functional, but maybe not aesthetically pleasing, filing system.

I called upon Nashville photographer Mary Rice to help me understand more about these kinds of images. She explained that naturally, everything depends upon the publication and the message that platform is trying to convey—or what they are trying to sell. Photographs like the ones in magazines may involve the combined efforts of an interior designer, art director, creative director, and/or a visual merchandiser before a photographer ever even walks into the room. The spaces are often, as you might suppose, shot in a staged studio—not an actual home or office.

Designers may spend a day or two setting up the room, tweaking the colors and objects for the desired effect. Once a photographer finally comes in to assess and adjust the lighting, they may shoot the same photo five to ten times from the same exact angle, and can spend hours editing to make the camera "see" in the same way the human eye does. From start to finish, the creation of "organized" photos can take anywhere from several hours to several days. Even if you're a pro at editing and filtering your own smartphone photos, you know they often project more or less what you want, as opposed to what is real.

Do you have the time and money to burn for the level of organizing perfection illustrated in those photos? What would that sort of perfection even get you? Yet do you feel some level of shame because your closet or desk looks a little different? Maybe it's not just different, but a completely overstuffed, out-of-control mess. If you're dealing with some heavy levels of disorganization, do these kinds of photos inspire or deflate?

What about a more practical depiction?

Before   After

Those are real-life photos, of a real-life closet. Does it seem attainable? Or at least realistic? The spaces depicted in the styled images do not, and cannot, exist in most realities, yet we frustrate ourselves attempting to replicate the labeled, the ordered, maybe even the minimalist home. Granted, the curated photos can be motivating and give you some great ideas. You can have pretty spaces that are also functional. But if you're not gifted organizationally, or are dealing with huge amounts of life disruption, getting things in order to that degree is just another pressure. It becomes defeating, expensive, and likely not even maintainable. The pressure to reach the standards of the photos may make you feel shame, or like you're just not good enough at organizing ever to get it exactly right.

Perhaps you've spent years pawing through piles of stuff to find what you need and have become accustomed to wasting tons of time moving items from one surface to another. Maybe you jumped on the latest organizing bandwagon with the highest of expectations, only to lose interest or backslide. Maybe it's even frightening to think about making a massive change in the way you handle stuff. Clutter and disorganization can become a comfortable way of life, at least on the surface. As a result, perhaps you stop before you even attempt to start, because being organized and consistently staying on top of things is a Big Scary Goal.

These paralyzing feelings and self-judgments do more than just keep us daydreaming on the couch. I've met plenty of people who won't invite anyone over to their home because of the clutter, others who won't invite clients into their offices because of the state of their desk and the piles of paper on the floor. Trying to get started with pulling things together in a more ordered way seems so out of reach and they often don't know where to begin. So, they're stuck. They may tell themselves that the fear is ridiculous, which naturally leads to more shame. Much to my shock, I've had business people who have called me for help only to be ridiculed by coworkers even as we're working together. I've watched family members shake their heads because a loved one can't seem to get things together and move forward. Where has this reaction ever been helpful to the person trying to improve? Shame is a scene-stealer in the disorganized life.

After years of attempts and few changes, it's often easier to give up and attempt to hide. Of course, you can hire someone else to come in and clear everything out, label everything, make it all pretty—without much of your direct input or commitment to the process. If someone else does it for you, it is definitely easier, and some people are able to maintain a system created by someone else. But this book isn't about that kind of situation.

Having someone else do the work without your investment is a little bit like hiring someone else to run a marathon for you. Where is the gratification if you don't actually take the steps, feel the exhaustion, and savor the exhilaration in crossing the finish line? Sometimes the process is difficult, painful, and tedious, but the journey of the marathon results in excellent lessons along the way—and maybe a few pulled or strained muscles, but there's learning in the uncomfortable things, too. Once you've run your marathon and gotten in shape, you have a chance to learn how to maintain and keep your balance. Maybe you will never even run another marathon, but you can make the commitment to keep that body moving, to take care of what you have. There is an eye-opening journey that can occur with this sort of commitment and persistence. Each time you get sidetracked from working on that Big Scary Goal, you have an opportunity to regain your balance, a chance to observe yourself and learn. How do I know?

Here is my story.

The Subplot: Sara's Big Scary Goal

> When I see an adult on a bicycle, I do not despair for the future of the human race.
>
> —H.G. Wells

If being organized and productive is difficult or uncomfortable for you, you're not alone—according to a 2013 IKEA Infographic titled "The State of Storage and Organization in US Homes," 43 percent of Americans consider themselves disorganized. And it's all well and good for me to preach about it, but I don't find it difficult or uncomfortable, at least not most of the time. My house isn't perfect, whatever that means. But when I want to get it close to perfect, I don't hesitate to purge, sort, and categorize. Give me a project or goal, and I'm all over laying out the sequential steps and details for getting it done. I was born with the linear-thinking, planner genes, so how on earth am I supposed to relate to anyone who struggles with maintaining order? Organizing for myself is an automatic process I don't even really think about. Thus, I needed a parallel, and, recognizing that there is always something we don't naturally excel at, I set out to define my own personal scene-stealing, unbalanced shame. After a little pondering, I think I have a corresponding Big Scary Goal.

I am one of the most naturally unathletic, sports-fearing individuals you will ever meet. To wit: It took a full two weeks of daily YMCA swim lessons for me to just put my head underwater. All the other kids were diving off the diving board by day four, and I never mastered anything more than a weak dog-paddle. All through grade school, I was the last kid picked for any team. No one wanted to do the three-legged race with me on field day. Like horses who sense fear from their riders, all the other kids seemed to know I was totally inept. I always missed the basket, got hit by the softball, closed my eyes when I swung a bat. I never passed the Presidential Physical Fitness Test. My elementary school gym teachers would shake their heads and tell my mother, "Bless her heart. At least she's a pretty good square dancer."

I joined the band in middle school, in part, to get out of gym classes for the rest of my school days—no sports for me. Over time, my defense mechanism was to become defiant in my shame over being utterly incompetent at catching a ball or running as fast as the pack. In college, as an education major, I was the only student I knew who received the lowest grades of their college experience in racquetball and weight lifting. It's always been incredibly uncomfortable for me to try to be athletic. But even as I tried to hide my lack of skills, I would watch the sporty kids and constantly compare myself to them. I so wished I was different.

One thing I did like to do very early in my childhood was ride a bike. I don't remember it being terribly hard for me to master, likely because it happened before I had learned much about fear. I had the basic little bike that my dad took the training wheels off of in due time when I was five or six, and I got around on it well enough. When I got a little older I asked for a ten-speed for my tenth birthday, because that's what all the other kids had. What I received was a very basic, plain blue bike with no gears or hand brakes. It was too big for me, so I could "grow into it," and it had one of those ridiculous white plastic baskets with flowers attached to the handlebars. Pragmatism was a big thing in our family.

But I think the primary reason I didn't get my request was because of an accident that happened involving my older brother Guy, something that scared the heck out of me at the time, and likely scared my parents more than I understood. He was nine years older than me, and I idolized him. When I was about four, he got his own ten-speed bike. Neither of my big brothers suffered the athletic ineptitude that I was cursed with, and Guy rode his bike easily and constantly—everywhere—that is, until the day he went flying down an ice-covered hill and lost control. Not only was Guy athletically gifted, but he also possessed a ridiculously calm demeanor in any situation, no matter how dire. After he came off the bike, skidded all over the pavement (these were pre-helmet days, remember), lost a fair amount of skin, and finally rolled to a stop, what did he do? He got up, and quietly walked himself and his battered bike half a mile home. I had the bad luck to barge in on him attempting to clean all the blood off in the bathroom sink—I'll spare you further detail on that. I know I was young, but I'll never forget what it felt like.

Four-year-old Sara: "Wh-wh-wh-what happened?!"

Thirteen-year-old Guy, shrugging: "I fell off the bike."

The injuries were of little consequence in his mind, but of course I shrieked like a banshee. I really think he would have been fine to slap a couple of Band-Aids on and call it good. Our parents disagreed. One trip to the emergency room, and somewhere between fifty and one hundred stitches later, we were all scarred. He returned home from the hospital covered in bandages and looking a bit like Frankenstein's monster—miraculously with no concussion or broken bones. I returned with a new awareness—you can get hurt on a bike. I'm guessing my parents had this new awareness as well.

Even so, my tenth-birthday bike was a new one—and shiny too—so I resolved to be grateful and get on with it. But there was another hitch. Being the child of overprotective parents who were now on red alert, I was never allowed to ride it onto the street. You read that right: I couldn't ever take my bike onto the street. It was "too dangerous." If I didn't fall or get run over, I was sure to be kidnapped. Mind you, by this time I was growing up in a very benign, middle-class neighborhood in the suburbs of Huntsville, Alabama. We lived toward the end of a street with a cul-de-sac and our backyard backed up to a huge cattle farm. The most dangerous thing that ever occurred there was one of the cows getting through the fencing and nosing around in someone's vegetable garden.

Despite the bucolic subdivision setting, I was restricted to wobbling unsteadily around in circles in our small driveway, where my mother could periodically check out the dining room window and be satisfied knowing that I would not be the next child needing a trip to the emergency room. As you might imagine, this activity quickly got old, and the bike eventually came to rest in a corner of the garage, destined to gather dust and provide an excellent home for spiders. I don't know what ever happened to it. I came to hate it and everything it represented.

I should pause here to say that my parents, God rest their souls, were really amazing people. They meant well, and I credit them with raising me in an atmosphere that supported much of my organizing know-how. But they were always waiting for the sky to fall. And frankly, if they hadn't been so overprotective, I might not have a book.

Fast-forward to my late twenties. My husband, Jeff, who is an avid cyclist, optimistically got me a really nice bike for the first birthday I had after we were married. It had gears. It had hand brakes. It was (is) red—the color I always wanted. I tentatively and unsteadily rode it around the streets of our neighborhood but never really ventured any further. It did not feel natural, I took a spill or two, and a weird little gripping fear kicked in and took hold. It, too, began to gather dust in our garage. The few cycling skills I had developed long before had apparently gone dormant, and thinking about riding a bike, and hopefully looking kind of confident and cool doing it, felt ridiculous and out of reach.

Aside: Although I am not athletically gifted, I do exercise. I'm still not quick or coordinated. I had a personal trainer once tell me I had no "fast-twitch" muscles. Whatever those are, I'm confident she was right. I do not compete in anything, in any way, but I have seasoned through running a few 5K road races, tennis lessons (two years and still can't play a game), golf lessons (the phrase "play through" was my mantra), tae kwon do classes (to keep my kids involved), a fair amount of weight training, and the errant aerobics class here and there. This is all to say I do recognize the importance of moving to be healthy, but none of it comes naturally to me, and consistency eludes me. The bike thing paralyzes me.

I also wholeheartedly believe that better organization equates to better health—but more on that later.

So, I will make you a deal, right here in the book. I'm going to try something that terrifies me a bit—scratch that—terrifies me a lot. As you wind your way through these chapters, I'm going to wind my way through training for, and completing, a sixty-two mile bike ride, also known as a "metric century."

Why the bike? I pondered a marathon, but for me, riding the bike is way more uncomfortable and packed with plenty of juicy emotional baggage. I want to feel the discomfort, the complete lack of confidence, the unsteadiness, and the overwhelm that I think some of you may feel when you look at a room packed with twenty-plus years of papers and unplanned purchases. And I would love for you to join me in setting your own Big Scary Goal. You see, riding a bike will mean not only getting ready physically, but:

- getting over the fear of sharing a road with large, four-wheeled things that don't even seem to notice me;

- getting over the fear of hitting the pavement and repeating a less exciting but equally painful version of my brother's experience (I'm kind of into self-preservation);
- getting over what my hair looks like when I take the helmet off (yes, this has been an excuse);
- getting over my butt hurting; and perhaps most importantly,
- getting over the truth that I will likely always be the slowest one, no matter what group I'm in or how much I train—I will never look the way I think a cyclist is supposed to look.

And what of you, you who do not believe you are gifted with an orderly, organized mindset? In order to progress with organization, you might need to:

- let go of the fact that you've let stuff slide for so long;
- release fear of what other people think;
- work through the questions of where to begin and how (you may already know some of those answers);
- rethink ideas of visual perfection in organization (or doing things the "right" way);
- move beyond the shame of having overbought or repurchased stuff you already owned; and
- let go of the past dropped balls, the missed appointments, and the lost items.

Note that this journey of mine has nothing to do with appearance, weight loss, or competition. I'm not going to count calories any more than I would weigh the bags of donations a client takes to charity. And I'm sure as heck not timing myself. I also acknowledge that conquering my anxiety with riding a bike may sound like an odd comparison to you finally clearing out a garage, but stick with me. The exercise is about moving through discomfort, fear, and perceived lack of ability—then seeing what can be done with the results.

How can we approach a Big Scary Goal in a way that perhaps doesn't fit with conventional wisdom, or the clever marketing ploys, but still gets us a level of competency that allows us to move forward? What is the value of working on something that feels so unnatural? I will never be in the Tour de France, and you may never be organizer of the year. So, what? I figure if I can make it through this ride, you can surely get rid of some stuffed animals and start regularly opening your mail. Shall we work through it together? I'll keep up my end of the bargain; you just have to make some forward motion and do a little thinking. How hard will it be? I haven't got a clue at this point, but only you and I can answer those questions for ourselves.

Here's where you might want to grab a pen or sticky notes or markers, whatever feels helpful.

Scribble:

- What or who are you comparing your organization, or lack thereof, to?
- What kind of fear or shame do you have about being more organized or managing your tasks more effectively?
- Are you open to setting a Big Scary Goal regarding organization and/or productivity? What could it be?

CHAPTER 2

Surrounded by Stuff, Nerves, and More Shame

The Story: Rachel*

Rachel, a work-outside-the-home mother of two, ushered me into her living room, self-consciously scooping up the school paper and cereal bowl fallout left from that morning, and shifting a stack of books off of the couch so I could have a place to sit. Rachel was nervous—fluttery, I sometimes call it, because that's how it looks, like a butterfly that just got disturbed by a curious toddler. She was hyper-aware of why I was there. She did invite me, after all, but I was probably the first person outside of her family that she had invited into her home in over a year. She was desperate to have a more tranquil, organized lifestyle, but she recently changed jobs and had to help her aging mother move out of her childhood home and into an Alzheimer's care facility six months before. Her garage was filled with furniture and memories that she couldn't bring herself to make decisions about at the time. Her house

---

* All "Story" characters are fictional.

was filled with other items she couldn't seem to make decisions about either.

Every time she thought she had a handle on things, something else popped up to derail her. Her spouse had not been particularly supportive—in his defense, he worked long hours, focused on getting school loans paid off. Although he thought she should just "use her time more wisely" and start picking up more, he did agree to her seeking some outside help.

We talked a bit so that she could settle and quit worrying about what I was thinking. And truly, I didn't think anything. I have a state of mind that I shift into when I walk into a disorganized situation that I can only describe as my robot mode, making observations and mental notes but not caring on any sort of emotional or judgmental level that the countertops aren't visible, or that there are unopened shopping bags piled in the corner, or that there's pet hair and Cheerios here and there on the floor. I was there to listen, assess, and support her in figuring out how to move forward.

We have so much to contend with in our twenty-first century lives. It's not fresh news that we are surrounded by the consequences of working more, buying more, committing to more. There are many reasons I started helping people with their surroundings in 2012, but I have to give partial credit to one book that inspired me to become an organizer. The title might surprise you: *Little House in the Big Woods*, by Laura Ingalls Wilder. The book perhaps romanticizes a pretty rough nineteenth-century lifestyle, but when I was a kid, I read it over and over again. I was fascinated with the differences between life in the 1800s and my own. As I read it to our own daughter in her elementary years, a new observation blew me away when I reread the passages about preparations for winter. Wilder describes in fine detail her mother gathering and storing the root vegetables in the cellar. Ma Ingalls organized onions and peppers and hung them in their attic, separating them from the categorized groupings of other staples. The pantry had plenty of cured items and cheeses to get them through until spring.

Following that description comes the tale of the butchering of the hog—both a community social event and a necessary methodical process, in which no part of the animal was wasted. Even the bladder was blown up and used as a toy, the tail fried as a special once-a-year treat for the little Ingallses, and of course, Jack the bulldog.

Here's what struck me: Planning for winter, organizing supplies, and preparing ahead of time for the Ingalls family was not a productivity hack, but a tool necessary for survival. Sure, there were limited resources, which in turn limited choices. Who knows how things might have been different if Pa had been a railroad baron instead of a homesteader? Still, nothing was overlooked, mindlessly discarded, or unnecessarily purchased. Essential items were arranged in such a way that nothing would go missing. I don't recall any descriptions of Mary misplacing her schoolbooks or Ma purchasing extra calico only to find a big stash already in the cedar chest. Delayed gratification was a given, not something they had to consciously teach in a world filled with one-click purchases. Now most of our complaints and struggles in getting ready for winter involve things like whether or not the kids have outgrown their coats, or if the in-laws are showing up for the holidays, or maybe whether we have to cut back a little to keep the credit card bill down. I think even as a kid I must have subconsciously admired and wanted to somehow emulate the survival-skill organizational doctrine of Ma Ingalls (minus living in rural Minnesota).

Let's get back to our mom, Rachel. Rachel was a paralegal, very well respected, and could hold things together pretty well at her new job. When she came home, she would fall apart because she felt safer letting her normal mode of being scattered manifest itself. Plus, between work, family, and her mother, she was exhausted.

As Rachel's children moved out of elementary and into middle school, contrary to her expectations, they seemed to require more of her time than when they were totally dependent upon her. When they started school, she went back to work. But then came the extracurriculars and the pressure to make sure her kids kept up with the pack. There was also the homework that occasionally required her assistance, the signing of forms, the checks and fees for various items, the discussions about friends and insecurity and life. She was routinely asked to volunteer for school events, and she tried to as much as possible. That's what good moms do, right? She also underestimated the energy assisting her mother would take away from her on a daily basis.

She was surrounded by choices and commitments that seemed to constantly limit her potential in the home. She rarely said no.

Whether parents should work or stay at home, or some combination of the two, is such an individual decision and so different for every family's situation. I acknowledge that for many of us it's a fact of life we have to contend with. But when we commit to it, something, or several somethings, has to give, and many times it ends up being the organization, time management, and overall internal efficiency of the household.

When the house falls into disorder, you might feel guilty and incompetent. You look the other way from the ever-growing piles of mail, and you don't let the kids have their friends over (never mind whether or not *you* have any friends). Stepping back from the scene, you might not recognize that you aren't the only one dealing with this kind of chaos. It's way more common than you think.

Sooner or later, the dust settles, you look around, and . . . holy crap. There is stuff—papers, pet toys, spare change, bottles of sunscreen, party favors, clothing that still has tags, ten boxes of light bulbs, permanent markers, etc., etc., etc.—everywhere. Did you need all of this? Did you buy something because you couldn't find the something you already had? And then when the soccer practice gets canceled and you have to leave work early to pick your child up, it blows up the time you thought you had to get the basics of organization handled.

This unbalanced lifestyle is a long way from the Big Woods, or maybe even from the lifestyle of your parents or grandparents. You don't have to worry about surviving a Minnesota winter sans electricity in 1882, but couldn't you be living a little easier? What mental skills did we trade off when rushing to the grocery store or whizzing through a drive-through replaced butchering the hog and drying the veggies? Fast solutions don't always serve us particularly well when we have to deal with the big stuff, the scary things like suddenly having to care for a parent, deal with a job loss, or navigate a divorce. In survival mode, we very often don't have time or mental space to plan ahead. We don't have much to fall back on to help us maintain our balance.

And what good does being nervous and embarrassed about our homes do for us? I took a very informal poll online about getting ready for guests in the home. 16.5 percent of participants in the survey would not invite someone into their home for dinner due to the stress involved.

As I talked to Rachel, I realized that statistic rang pretty true for her. Sadly, disconnection compounded the problem. She had lost her way with the baseline organizational practices that she thought everyone else had all figured out, and it was nerve wracking to think about anyone else seeing her spaces. Work-life balance was not on her radar at this stage of life, and I just wanted to give her a hug and tell her it was all OK. I didn't (because I didn't want to freak her out even more), but I did explain to her that it was not surprising that she got swept away by her circumstances, and that it would be possible to break through and regain the skills needed to manage her home more effectively.

Rachel had lots of thoughts and doubts swimming around in her brain. She hadn't previously considered the impact of her life events on her clutter. She wondered all sorts of things out loud as we walked and talked through her spaces:

- "Should I have bought some more bins?" (The answer was no.)
- "Will I have to let go of a lot of stuff?" (That depends.)
- "What about this room over here?"
- "If I get organized, what if I can't *stay* organized?"

The last one is a perfect question, because backsliding happens all the time. Developing the ability to maintain doesn't happen overnight, or by reading a two-minute article titled "10 Quick Ways to be Organized." You can learn to be more organized, but it will likely take some time and experimentation until you can figure out systems that work specifically for you. Actually, I believe that's what you must do for long-term success, because organization is not one-size-fits-all. Did Ma Ingalls organize her attic just like all of the other frontier women? Did she take time to store vegetables cleverly and in ROYGBIV order? I suspect she utilized a combination of following her own mother's lead, recognizing what worked for her family, and a healthy dose of intuition. Where's our intuition when it comes to creating order for ourselves?

Part of my job is assuring people that there is always a way forward for anyone, no matter how far down they've gone, to improve their organization. So after Rachel shared her story, I asked her which area was giving her the most heartburn. She had no idea. "Please fix everything," she said quietly.

Using my own intuition, I suggested that we move into the mudroom by the back door. We started to sort the shoes, backpacks, and school paperwork, and began the slow but steady process of making some sense of it all.

The Subplot: My First Cycle Class

I was pretty nervous because I signed up for this intro to cycling class at the gym we belong to. I figured I needed to get a better level of fitness before I headed out on the open road. Actually, it was kind of an excuse to *not* get out on the open road—but you know, baby steps. My husband Jeff and I had gone out the night before to get the requisite padded bike tights. Those things are not flattering. I was perplexed about whether or not I needed the shoes with those clip things, so we decided I should wing it and wear my regular cross-training shoes.

I had been making some feeble attempts at working out, but I knew I was not in fabulous shape. I had been heavy into doing this entrepreneur thing, I reasoned. I confessed to myself that I was worried about what the instructor and other attendees would think. My heart rate increased just contemplating walking into the room. I had been researching group rides and training programs in the area. Jeff was eager to assist, and I appreciated his support, but I wasn't sure about how I felt about his advice. At this point I had no clue where this journey was going. I hadn't fleshed out how I wanted things to be; I just knew that I wanted to not be terrified on a bike. I was sure he had lofty plans for me—but the metric century idea comes along much later in this story. I did think I needed a Big Scary Goal to shoot for, something that would push me and get me outside my comfort zone, something that would teach me some lessons I'd either forgotten or never learned in the first place. I was leaning toward a fifty-mile ride that coincided with my upcoming fiftieth birthday. Was it synchronicity, or a sign? It seemed insurmountable, with so many years between me and a bike. I felt more than a little awkward and ridiculous that riding a bike seemed like such a scary goal.

When I was a little kid and learned how to ride my first small bike—I have a vague recollection of this—my dad took off the training wheels and, holding the back of the seat, ran along behind me as I pedaled. I have no clue when his hand finally came off and I found balance on my own. But then I just rode—in rain, in heat, up and down the street in front of our house—without any sort of self-consciousness. It was that simple, and it was instinctive. When our own children learned how to ride (and how ironic is it that I helped them to learn?), it was a similar experience. Other than the bikes and their helmets, we didn't buy anything special. I didn't even have a helmet when I learned. Now when it's a little hot or cold outside, we all head to the gym for cycling class, complete with heart rate monitors and weird shoes.

I often tell clients that they cannot buy their way into better organization. Having cool organizing stuff is fun, but it can't make decisions or take donations to the thrift store for them, and the same principle applies to cycling. There's a great book out there that helped me put some of the learning-to-ride process into a more realistic perspective; it's called *Just Ride*, by Grant Petersen, and I highly recommend it for anyone wanting to get out more on a bike. It's a no-frills, get-busy-and-do-it manual that does a nice job of dispelling some myths about cycling, like the idea that you have to have certain equipment or a special wardrobe. I wish I'd found it much earlier in this journey. I never wanted to get caught up in following what everyone else is doing because, frankly, I can't do what everyone else does. If I could, I wouldn't be writing this story.

But I wasn't even close to actually riding the bike at this point.

I arrived at the class early, as always. The cycling class instructor was very understanding when I gave her a few details about my situation. She was helpful and sympathetic to my plight. I relaxed, just a bit. She appeared to have never had any issues with either gaining muscle mass or building her cardio, but she listened carefully to my goals, and she helped me to have some hope. There was no pressure or judgment. She assisted me in setting the seat level and adjusting the height and distance of the bars. Shoes with clips might have been helpful but were definitely not essential. I bravely hopped on the bike, determined to follow her every step. I had so much to remember and to focus on.

I mentally beat myself up a few times before class started, just for good measure. Others entered the room, and I instantly felt like I was being assessed. I was feeling awkward and weak, and totally out of familiar territory, but I managed to get started. It was difficult for me to grasp how this experience might help me achieve my goal, so I simply clung to whatever the instructor shouted into her mike as the music cranked up. I kept my eyes forward, and I spoke to no one.

I survived, but I was still pretty distrustful of myself. I hoped nobody was paying attention to me or noticing that I wasn't always turning up the tension knob when I was supposed to. I also couldn't stop thinking that, even though the class was good for me, it wasn't the same as actually riding a bike on a road. Pedaling to nowhere in a dark room led by someone shouting through a headset (over the bass turned up to eleven) might help me get those quads up to speed, but it was a far cry from my original vision for riding a bike. How would I ever make the connection? Could I make the switch to the real thing?

It was a start. I made a plan to keep going.

Scribble:

- What do you hide due to disorganization?
- When was the last time you followed your instincts about where to store something, or whether or not to discard something?
- What makes you nervous about letting others in on your organizing challenges?

CHAPTER 3

We All Fall Down

> Life is like a ten-speed bicycle. Most of us have gears we never use.
>
> —Charles M. Schulz

The Story: Dylan

Every day you get up with the steely resolve to tick off that to-do list, clear out the closet, or get the bags of outgrown clothing out of the garage. But every day something gives you pause, holds you back, and stops your progress. After the first fifteen to thirty minutes or so of attempting to organize a space, you feel indecisive, bored, or incompetent, and sit staring at the packed drawers and cabinets, immobile and ineffective. There are more interesting, less stressful things to do with your time, at least at that particular moment. Maybe you head off to hang with a friend, reasoning that tomorrow is another day and after all—what's another twenty-four hours?

You may think you know what it takes to get organized because it seems like it should be such a simple process. Just clear out the clutter. Ask yourself if the item is beautiful or useful. Use the one-in-one-out rule. That's all solid advice, but why haven't those techniques worked for you so far? For one thing, there is a distinction to be made between decluttering and organizing. They are two separate activities that happen to work well together, but they are not the same thing. For another, sometimes you can be exposed to a message over and over, but until a complete stranger steps in and assesses the situation, you don't accept it.

So it was when I entered Dylan's office. Dylan was a successful thirty-something real estate agent. Energetic and witty, he fretted through years of wondering why he couldn't seem to keep a calendar straight or stay focused on important projects. His office was unsurprising for my line of work—stacks of paper on the desk, credenza, and floor; labeled bins in various sizes overflowing with books, brochures, and other marketing materials; scraps of paper covered in lists stuck everywhere. You could barely see his computer monitor. Because of the easygoing personality that camouflaged his intense drive, he was successful, but he never let his clients see how frantic he felt underneath it all. He already felt judged enough when colleagues walked past his office. He was fed up with the stress and eager to make some headway on creating new, more organized habits.

Prior to reaching out to me, Dylan tried a variety of methods to keep himself on track. He purchased every app or piece of productivity software he heard about and tried all of them at least once. Downloading is fun. The labeled bins were another attempt. They looked cool in the store, but once he got them in the office and put things in them, he never took anything back out. To heck with paying attention to labels. He ended up forgetting what supplies he already had and just ordered more.

At one point, Dylan even bravely allowed his super-organized sister, Haley, in to help him work through the piles. Haley, with the best of intentions, more or less staged an organizing intervention. The session didn't go quite as smoothly as either of them had planned. A hard-charging, type-A mother of five, she was repeatedly dumbfounded at how Dylan hadn't kept files in order and why it was so difficult for him to get things from his head or email messages to the calendar. She didn't hide any of her shock or attempt diplomacy any more than she had when they were thirteen and nine and she was chasing him out of her middle school slumber parties. In the end, although a lot of stuff was cleared out, the experience left him feeling defeated and concerned that something important had been tossed or placed somewhere he wouldn't remember.

I'm going to pause our story for a moment and remind you of four of the worst words a chronically disorganized person can hear: "Why can't you just . . ."

For example:

- "Why can't you just shred or scan all of the excess paper?"

- "Why can't you just remember to put things back where you got them?"
- "Why can't you just make a list, like *I* do?"
- "Why can't you just take five minutes at the end of each day to clear your desk off?"
- "Why can't you just put everything into your planner?"

Sometimes those words are delivered with a sincere desire to help, and I suspect Dylan's sister said some similar things. But imagine yourself on the receiving end—how does it feel? Unfortunately, in Haley's ill-fated attempt to be supportive, a document was accidentally thrown in the shredding that caused Dylan a fair amount of stress and trouble to recreate. Now, his fear of losing important paperwork was fierce, and the thought of trying to reorganize once again had him completely stuck. He had felt silly at first, but now he was frozen. And with his mess, he was hindering himself by not being as responsive to clients as he could or should be.

The mental torture of not feeling on top of all of the paperwork was a constant worry simmering in the back of his mind. He knew he wasn't working up to his potential. Why *couldn't* he "just" do this thing? Accepting assistance from his sister was difficult, and all it got him was a running tape of, "I can't do this. Organizing takes too much time, and it screws me up anyway . . ." looping in his head.

Asking for help isn't always such a rough experience. I had a conversation recently with a client—we'll call him Bob—who has been experiencing some astounding productivity success after receiving help. I won't take much credit—he is motivated and persistent, even with some stops and starts. If I could help all clients to the same level of success, I might just organize my way out of a job. So one day I asked, "What do you think made the difference for you this time around?" Bob responded, "I finally admitted to myself I needed the help, and asked for it. Admitting I needed it was tough. Asking for it was next to impossible, but from there on out, things got easier." It's always darkest before the dawn, and acceptance makes a difference. But in some cases, like Dylan's, it doesn't always pay to work with those closest to you.

So let's get back to that story. Dylan, of course, did decide to try again, and he reached out to me for organizing support. One of the first issues we tackled was digital. The files on his computer were less overwhelming and more approachable to him than the physical stuff. He had to compile a ton of documents for some due diligence on a commercial property, and the project allowed us to build up some trust and confidence before we moved back into actual paper. He had hundreds of files already saved on his computer, but the names were incomprehensible—things like "PcAL12_345Oville.doc." There were numerous duplicates, folders labeled incongruently, and hundreds of random subfolders. No wonder he couldn't find anything. In attempts to get organized he had let the system—several systems, actually—get ahead of the content, something I refer to as letting process get in the way of product.

I pointed at the above-mentioned file name and asked, "What *is* that document anyway?" He replied that it was a copy of a recorded deed for one portion of a larger property. "OK," I said, "So if you were going to search or ask for the deed at the county office, what would you call it?"

Small epiphany, here. Dylan would search for the deed for Parcel A of Lot 12, 34 Smith Lane in Orderville. So, we renamed the file "ParcelALot1234SmithLaneOrderville."

Dylan looked at me skeptically, observing, "That's a really long file name."

"Who cares how long the name is? Name a file what you would call it," I responded. He laughed and allowed himself a sigh of relief. Now he knew what it was and where to find it. It would also pop up in searches more easily.

We started reviewing all of the digital files, renaming things in a way that made contents crystal clear and deleting duplicates or obsolete documents. Everything related to that particular sale went into one folder, not twenty. The work was time consuming on the front end, sure, but hopefully a tremendous time saver going forward if he kept up the naming convention. We discussed how to prevent the same issues going forward. Working together on digital issues opened up enough trust for us to move on to the piles of paperwork, and he even figured out his own method for capturing notes that eliminated enough sticky notes for him to view his screen.

I never wondered why he couldn't already organize something, even if it seemed obvious. What difference would that make? I wanted to, help him figure out what would make the most sense for him going forward. I did say some things he had heard before, some things he probably already knew and realized were correct. But maybe hearing someone else verify that his instincts were headed the right way made some difference. Maybe even hearing several things his sister had already suggested was confirmation that there was indeed a method to this madness.

Whatever the difference was, after several sessions, Dylan's systems—they belonged to him, after all, not me—took hold and spread. Recognizing that he relished the feeling of being more in control of his surroundings, he started reorganizing and clearing out his car more frequently. He even sent me some pictures of a supply closet he worked on at home. Finally realizing that you can come up with ways to organize, and feel some authority and peace, can become a little addictive when your confidence builds.

Lest you think this is all a big advertisement for hiring professional organizers, I can assure you that there are many ways to seek assistance. Just because Dylan's sister wasn't a big help doesn't mean that you can't work with any family member (see Chapter 7) or find a nonjudgmental, compassionate friend to support you.

Maybe you can even have someone simply be present with you, someone who doesn't necessarily organize with you but serves as an anchoring presence for your work. Maybe you chat; maybe you work on things in parallel; maybe you ask them to check in with you from time to time. This concept is known as body doubling, and it works well for many people when they struggle to stay on task.

Alternatively, you might just need someone to handle a portion of the process, like taking away things that need to be shredded or donated. Maybe you have a friend with an itching label-maker finger that would love to help. Perhaps you need someone to affirm your instincts, to just say, "Yes, it's fine to throw away the Christmas cards from 2005. No one will hold it against you."

You can access a variety of nonhuman resources as well, recognizing that different people respond to different delivery systems for assistance. Books, videos, TV shows, blogs, and podcasts can provide support and inspiration. Doing it all on your own may seem like the best way to keep your disorganization a secret—and maybe you think you *should* be able to do it on your own. But when you're stuck, does it really matter how you regain your momentum?

The Subplot: On the Road Again

Hiding out in the cycle class was apparently not enough. It seemed I needed to ride on actual streets to achieve my goal. Over the past several years I'd gone up and down the street in our neighborhood a few times, ventured into an empty parking lot, and ridden on a local greenway, an excursion during which I ran squarely into one of my children, fell and scraped my leg, and got a flat tire. As a cyclist, I've bounced between being a quivering heap of fear and being an actual menace to others on the road. Has anyone complained about me? Did I hinder someone else's progress because I was slow and entirely out of practice?

Or did that even matter? Did I hinder *myself* because I was slow and out of practice? Would it be better to keep working it at the gym before I unleashed myself on the unsuspecting public? Maybe after just another week of classes I wouldn't be afraid anymore. Or maybe I was not cut out for this whole idea. Why would I do this to myself when there were so many other less demanding pursuits? The mind games began.

Jeff and I decided to set out very early one morning so I could get used to the street again without the distraction of traffic. I was wobbly and, as always, slow. We spent just under an hour riding around our subdivision, including the sleepy cul-de-sacs and the busier main thoroughfare. Jeff was patient with my intermittent freak-outs. I encountered precisely four cars, three runners, a dozen or so other cyclists on a group ride, and one man walking a puppy. They all unnerved me in varying degrees, but I was determined to get used to this business of maneuvering around other things—some of which, unfortunately, moved too. I felt like the other cyclists we saw were all scoffing at me, judging my lack of cycling coolness. I knew I didn't look like they did on a bike, and it wasn't because of the way I was dressed or because I didn't have the same sort of bike. Still, a few more of these excursions took place over the course of several weeks, and I made some creeping, but respectable, progress.

But then, as a good-faith gesture and measure of encouragement, we purchased a new road bike that I clearly hadn't earned yet. Going up hills on my old bike was challenging because it was heavy, and it wasn't really cut out for my long distance goal. I christened my new set of wheels "Flo," because I decided that if I could just rediscover the flow I had in early childhood, I would be able to do this thing. Also, we name everything at our house—cars, key pieces of furniture, space heaters, etc.—perhaps that's another book. She was beautiful, teal and white, and sleek. She had things like disc brakes and I don't even know how many speeds. I could lift her with one hand. She was way more than I had dreamed of back in third grade, and I hoped I could earn her respect. Jeff, once again, got up very early on a Sunday morning (not his natural inclination) to offer his support on my first real road adventure with Flo. I refused to wear the cycling jersey we bought because it didn't seem like I had accomplished enough yet for a jersey. I barely thought I deserved the bike.

Flo has clipless pedals, which is a stupid term because they actually do have clips, and there's a fairly long story connected with the whole nomenclature that I won't bore you with. Whatever they're called, I was supposed to learn to clip in and clip out, and this ability would make me a finely-tuned, aerodynamic cycling machine. I had done this clipping business in the cycling class, so I supposed this all made sense. When I test rode Flo at the shop, I wore regular shoes, and the pedals had not been switched out for the shoes with cleats. Jeff assured me at the time that making the transition would be no biggie as cyclists do this all the time. My intuition suspected otherwise. Still, we switched the pedals and ventured out.

On the Sunday morning in question, I bravely started with my left foot firmly on a curb and my right foot slipped into the clip. I pushed off. I couldn't get my left foot clipped. I got distracted and nervous, and I fell—hard. I scraped my knee up a little and pissed myself off. I tried again and was able to keep going this time. But unclipping and stopping? What was I thinking? I hit the brakes before either foot was out, fell again, and scraped the same knee up even worse. I really had no clue how to accomplish this feat of balance and coordination. Now the fear was really kicking in—sweaty palms, racing heartbeat, totally tensed mobility—and although I kept riding, it got to the point where I couldn't even start myself without Jeff holding the handlebars steady until I felt I could move forward and pedal. We were quite a sight in the neighborhood. Small children emerged from their backyards to stare with pity at the bloody-kneed crazy lady who couldn't even ride her bike. The shame was reaching a middle-school era level of awkwardness.

Jeff was patient but clearly baffled at my inability to master this, for him and many others, incredibly simple step. "Why can't you just put your foot in the clip and go?" That may not have been his exact sentence, but the sentiment was there. And either way, it's what my ears heard.

I would love to tell you that with just a few more attempts I had the whole thing figured out, but you know better. More falling occurred. If I had had the good sense to search the Internet for "riding with clipless pedals" ahead of this misadventure, I would have found plenty of articles that would have dissuaded me from trying it so soon. Guess what? Most everyone falls a few times, including experienced cyclists. What was I doing complicating my efforts by attempting to do it the way everyone else supposedly does it? After all, is the point to ride a bike, or get my foot in a vise-like grip that mentally paralyzes my ability to move my feet up and down? Couldn't it be more approachable to figure out my own way, a simplified way that makes sense for me?

And what about this familial thing? Many people can learn things from a loved one, but lots of people, like Dylan and me, get defensive. It's like when the accomplished piano teacher tries to work with her own kids and everyone ends up throwing the sheet music and storming off in tears. I got touchy and grumpy when Jeff was helping me—unfairly so. It is what it is.

I decided to look for my own third-party intervention. I needed someone to teach me a few things in a stranger's objective voice. I needed to ask for help.

Scribble:

- Have you sought help for your organizing or productivity challenges? Who did you ask or what resource did you use?
- What can you learn from the experience, even if, or especially if, it wasn't successful?
- If you haven't looked for help, what are some resources you could explore?

CHAPTER 4

Who's Judging Who?

"It is sad that we settle for the short-run effectiveness of shaming people instead of the long-term life benefits of grace-filled transformation. But we are a culture of progress and efficiency, impatient with gradual growth."

–Richard Rohr, "Change as a Catalyst for Transformation," *Daily Meditations*

The Story: Patrick

Before we begin this story, a little background context is in order.

Lack of organization in the workplace can be a tricky thing because it exposes some pretty personal tendencies in a very public way. As I mentioned in the introduction, I've been startled several times to notice people in an office environment picking on a disorganized colleague. I don't ever tell others in the office why I'm there, but somehow word often gets out, mostly because my client decides to be brave and open about it. They make a few cracks about someone going missing in the paperwork on the desk; then they smile at me like I'm going to commend them for pointing out their coworker's shortcomings. The subliminal message is, "See, I'm the organized one. I'm sure you'll like and approve of me." Or, even more insidious, "I can't believe she is actually paying someone just to help her file paperwork! What a loser." Like that's all there is to it.

Doing what I do, I get a weird window on the world sometimes. At parties or gatherings, if someone finds out my occupation, I often get amusing, and sometimes even troubling, comments. Things along the lines of:

- "Wow, my [husband/wife/mom/dad/son/niece/best friend] sure could use you—they're a wreck! Do you offer gift certificates?"
- "I am super organized! I love organizing! I've read [*Popular Organizing Book*] three times, and I know where everything is in my house! I used to organize all my friends' toys when I was little! I have three different label makers."
- "I'll bet you see horrible things! What's the worst place you've ever worked in? Do you see all that stuff like on the TV shows?"
- "I still have my [stuffed animal/comic book/action figure/baseball card] collection from when I was a kid—and I'll never get rid of them because some of them are really valuable."

All of these sorts of statements really boil down to one thing—people I don't even know seem to care quite a bit about what my impression is of them from an organizational standpoint. Occasionally I even have to remind friends and family that have known me for years, for way longer than I've actually been organizing professionally, that when I come over to their home I am not sizing up their kitchen drawers or assessing the state of their bookshelves—unless, of course, they invite me to. We are all uptight to either impress with or hide from our natural tendencies for the sake of first impressions. I suppose I've been guilty of freaking out myself when someone tells me their occupation: I'm very conscious when I meet a hair stylist, for instance, especially on days when I didn't even bother to blow mine dry.

But back to the office.

At various times during my various careers, I've had some pretty disorganized colleagues and bosses. People who were truly unable to balance their time and demands, perplexed about how to handle a workflow, how to delegate, or how to plan ahead. Details were not their strong suit, and everyone in the office suffered for it. I'll admit I complained sometimes, either because I had to put out a fire caused by their disorganization or just because it drove me crazy. I recall years ago a coworker half-jokingly challenged me to organize their workspace, which I did with a vengeance. The results lasted less than a month, and they were proud to show me that the efforts weren't worthwhile. This event occurred years before I was organizing professionally, and I would know better than to take the bait now.

I don't recall berating any of these people in person, but it certainly could have happened. I know that many of them probably secretly wished to be more organized but didn't have a clue about where to start. Planning out the details of a project or routinely cranking through a to-do list was not in their wheelhouse. Rather than exhibit any sign of weakness, some of these colleagues gave up and became what I call defiantly disorganized, the "You can't make me clean off this nightmare of a desk because I'm a busy and important person!" kind of disorganized. Some of them had told themselves that the chaos was actually a sign of success, because if the desk was clear, it must mean that they had nothing important to do, no business, no busyness.

Then, too, the concept of working with someone to assist with organization and productivity wasn't as well known, not to mention a lack of awareness that different brains organize differently. Now I wonder if some of them would continue to scoff and pile the files or if they might open themselves up for some help. Does it exhibit weakness to try to make some changes by enlisting the help of someone else?

At the urging of his spouse, Patrick called me into his office to assist with his desk and the surrounding space. Patrick was one of the co-owners of a healthcare company, used to projecting an in-charge, C-suite kind of vibe. His entrepreneurial spirit and people skills made up for, but did not entirely obscure, the massive stacks of files on his desk and his tendency to be fifteen to twenty minutes late to every meeting, or to miss them altogether. He had a very patient and very organized assistant who was, unfortunately, planning to retire soon after our scheduled sessions were completed. Patrick's wife could sense what might be coming down the pike when Patrick's main administrative support disappeared.

I offered to meet Patrick at an off time, when fewer coworkers would be around to peek in and see what was going on. He was guarded about the whole situation and felt like he didn't deserve the extra assistance. It's twisted, but many of my clients think they should become more organized *before* they meet with me, like going to the doctor with a broken ankle but making a good-faith effort of resting, icing, and putting weight on it first. Again, those first-impression anxieties get in the way.

Despite our discretion, two employees caught on to my visit and stopped to smirk through the glass wall of Patrick's office. I thought it was pretty brazen, considering he was the boss of most of the people in the building. We'd only just started the session, so it looked as if we had just created more chaos by unstacking everything to designate categories—you generally have to create some mess to fix some mess. Exchanging knowing looks, they sauntered off to the break room, and Patrick, being extremely perceptive and sensitive, visibly shrank down in his chair. He tried to joke, "Yeah, I'm like the exotic zoo animal on display around here." But the pain was evident, and he was getting frustrated as it registered that we wouldn't get through everything in one session. He knew I wouldn't be able to magically wave an organizing wand and make the pain all go away in one fell swoop.

I sensed that fear and shame were creeping into the situation, and I asked him if we could regroup and chat for a minute. Patrick was dejected, but he agreed. I could see that he was wondering if any of our time together had been worth it. What kind of an organizer was I, anyway? With the space and his disorganized role in it, after all, it was almost too much of a Big Scary Goal. Why should he even try? Couldn't he just turn it all over to someone else?

I started our conversation by asking him if he was right- or left-handed.

He looked puzzled. "Left?" he said.

"And how tall are you?"

More puzzlement. "Six-two."

I took a moment to look around the recently cleared surfaces, because up until that point we had only been able to deal with the mounds of files. We'd separated out a medium-sized forest of recycling and shredding. I noticed that everything remaining on the desk was situated as follows: the office phone to the left; a pad of paper, pen cup, and coaster for a drink to the right. A large printer occupied a right return on the desk with the paper tray facing the opposite wall. The arrangement meant that Patrick had to put down his ever-present coffee on the right side, reach to the left for the phone with his right hand, and then try to cross over to the pen and paper with his left in order to jot something down while on the phone.

If he needed to print anything or reload the machine, he either stood up and leaned his tall self all the way over the desk, or walked around to the other side, which didn't feel natural or instinctive. Usually, he just delayed picking up what came off the printer and would often reprint something he had forgotten already existed in the tray. Sometimes the papers would overflow and end up on the floor. He kept stacking the paperwork in the empty desk surface on the left, because his main file drawer was the one lowest to the floor on the right, an uncomfortable reach.

Lying underneath the piles of stuff that had gathered over time, this off-kilter arrangement wasn't evident to him. He just always had the underlying sense that his desk was uncomfortable, so he avoided maintaining it. He often picked up a stack or two of files and his laptop, and took them to a conference room to work. We rearranged everything, even his desk chair, to better fit his left-handedness and height, starting with turning the printer around and moving the phone to the right. Testing this arrangement out, suddenly a look of surprised relief—even hope—came over his face.

Being comfortable in a space you spend a tremendous amount of time in is really an under-appreciated, critical detail. I talk with clients about something I call "barriers to maintenance," which are annoying things that dissuade us from keeping up with organization. A barrier to maintenance could be a drawer that doesn't slide smoothly or a shelf placed slightly too high. Sometimes, it's the tiniest of irritations that become barriers, like a closet door that won't close all the way or an obstinate lid on a bin. Sometimes it's just a complicated process, like having to go through a huge collection of email folders and subfolders to find that one critical message. I identified a barrier once when I realized that I wasn't putting cups back into a cabinet just because an errant vine on a houseplant kept getting in the way of closing the door. It was small, but that's the kind of obstacle that can snowball left unchecked. And yes, I moved the plant. If something isn't ridiculously and intuitively easy to retrieve from and return to its best home, it's probably not going to stay organized.

One person's barrier to maintenance might be totally different from another's. For instance, I adore velvet-covered hangers because to me they look uniform, clothes don't slide off, they don't make dents in the shoulders, and they don't warp. Those hangers encourage me to keep the closet straight. But I know clients who absolutely won't use them precisely because clothing *won't* slide on and off easily. I even had someone tell me they just didn't like seeing lint collect on the velvet. In an effort to unconsciously avoid their dislike of the hangers, everything eventually ended up in a pile on the floor. It doesn't matter whether the barrier seems trivial or not; if it prevents you from sticking with your system—in any way, shape, or form—it needs to be re-evaluated and resolved.

Developing awareness of your own unique brand of barriers is key. When your system doesn't feel instinctive, or if you're noticing that it's taking several steps to keep stuff in place, stop and think. Step back and see if you can identify what is troublesome, annoying, or uncomfortable. When Patrick started attentively looking and feeling his way around the office, he became more aware of his physical requirements and preferences, and that he was in charge of the arrangement of his stuff. Having that sense of control was just the boost he needed to encourage continued progress toward his organizing balance, and to feel comfortable with the length of time it might take to attain that balance. He was no longer organizing to fight against what others thought. He was organizing for his own success.

The Subplot: Who Could Possibly Fix Me?

If someone makes an appointment with me, they are, in a sense, forced to deal with the organizing or productivity challenges they've been experiencing. I often hear, "I know how to do this thing, but I just won't unless you're here." My showing up and standing there looking at the space with them spurs action, through some subtle pressure that isn't present when they are alone.

Sometimes, what is not being said out loud is, "I'm paying you money to help me with this problem, and that's on top of the money I wasted buying all of this crap. I have to make the most of this time so I don't feel even worse about throwing good money after bad."

Throwing good money after bad. That sounds negative. What if we changed the word "money" to "energy" in that idiom? " ...so I don't feel worse about throwing good energy after bad [energy]." Put that way, it seems like it would be a positive thing to be throwing some good energy around, wouldn't it?

Once someone spends money on something it sends a message. It might say:

- This item is a basic need.
- This item or service will make me feel better.
- Clicking "purchase" or "buy" is exciting, and I need excitement.
- I'm in a hurry, and this item will meet my immediate need.
- I'll be healthier if I buy this item.
- I've saved for this item or service, and I deserve it.

Or any other number of justifications, some of which are understandable and reasonable.

Once someone has expressed the desire to reach an organizing goal, I believe that it sends out an energetic message. That message might be:

- I think my space could look, sound, smell, feel like . . .
- If I actually accomplish this goal, I will be different.

- I want to be different.
- I'm sick of living this way.
- I want my space to show people who I am.
- I want my space to support me in who I am.
- I want to set a good example.

When I set out to be a better bike rider, or any sort of bike rider, I needed to articulate that goal to myself and others (which was scary). I had to learn what was needed, plan out my time, experience the process, evaluate my progress, and then finish what I started. I needed to put some good energy into the journey, but I also suspected that I needed someone else to spend that energy on and with. I might not have done any of it without backup.

Sometimes, having someone help means connecting with a complete stranger and opening up to scrutiny. I searched all over Nashville for bike training classes, to no avail. I was thinking it was a missed business opportunity until I had one stroke of luck or, perhaps, divine intervention. When Jeff and I went to a local bike shop to get my pedals switched back (I finally convinced him), I saw a stack of business cards for something called Bike Fun.

Bike lessons. And fun—fun was in the mix too. It was, apparently, not an oxymoron, but an answer from the universe. Sometimes my clients tell me that right about the time they started pondering asking for some organizing or productivity help, someone told them about me, or my blog came up on their feed, or they heard me speak somewhere—synchronistic things do happen. The next day I reached out and contacted the founder and owner, KJ Garner, and almost immediately backpedaled (no pun intended). I wondered what I was getting myself into.

We exchanged a few email messages. After KJ got some preliminary information, she scheduled our first lesson right away. I have to say that, despite knowing that I had willingly set the plan in motion, I had serious anxiety, starting a few days prior to our first lesson when she emailed me to confirm. I had repeated visions of freezing up, falling, failing. You seasoned riders out there probably cannot relate to this apprehension at all, and I recognize wholeheartedly the weirdness of my self-professed cyclophobia.

The morning of the first lesson, with no small amount of trepidation, I managed to hook our bike rack to the back of my Subaru, wrestle Flo onto it, and get her strapped on. I was reasonably confident I'd done it right, but even if I hadn't, I only had a mile or so to go—the irony that I was driving a mile to ride a bike in a parking lot is not lost on me.

I pulled up in the designated deserted lot we had selected, and KJ was already there. It is unusual for someone to actually beat me to an appointment, so I was already caught off guard. She had set up halved tennis balls in the lot in a nightmarish obstacle course. She was wheeling around on her bike easily and effortlessly. I felt my heart pounding, and then I noticed it—she was wearing a green tutu. I got out, introduced myself, and she asked if I wanted my tutu as well—magenta, if memory serves. She had brought one for me, because on her client intake form I noted that the one word that described my feeling on a bike was "tense." Apparently, tutus are relaxing. I calmly informed her I hadn't earned the right to wear a tutu just yet, and she accepted my rejection gracefully. I decided we were off to a decent start.

She asked me to hop on (like it was so easy) and ride wherever and however I wanted, so she could see what was going on. I was furtively glancing around to see if anyone else was watching—to stare at me and mock me. There was only a park maintenance truck on the far side of the lot, and the guy inside appeared to be snoozing. The place looked empty otherwise, so it seemed I was safe.

Somehow, I managed to start pedaling and wobble for a few yards, feeling like a cross between Pee-wee Herman and someone in one of those T. rex costumes with the short little arms. "Oh, and did I mention, KJ, that I can only make left turns?" I said, with what I hoped sounded like casual indifference. Right turns, inexplicably, terrified me (that, too, has a name—dextramophobia). I felt like I was going to throw up from my lack of confidence and my concern that KJ would pack up her surgically-altered tennis balls in disgust and leave me to my foolishness.

A keen and calm observer, KJ was unperturbed. The first thing she noticed was the height of my seat. Producing a set of tools from thin air, she went to work. It was like she was the Mary Poppins of biking instructors, pulling out all sorts of amazing things at random moments and making it all go down easily.

It was astounding how such a small change made such a huge difference. By lowering the seat two centimeters, I was suddenly more secure. My feet were closer to the ground, and I was more stable and, hey—balanced! Even though we sized and adjusted things at the shop when we bought Flo, the seat was out of whack; the original height would have been appropriate for someone ready to race, but that someone was not me. My husband and the guy at the store had high hopes for me. Touching, really, that they thought I could handle it. I felt weird about it at the time, but I didn't want them to think I was a wimp. So I didn't say anything. I wanted them to think I was as confident as they imagined me to be.

Once KJ made this adjustment, I could finally start and stop on my own again. I was centered, and I felt a sense of control over my bike that I hadn't felt in a long time. I relaxed. I still had to start with my butt in the seat, not the way she was hoping I'd push off, but I felt more confident already. Thrilled and excited, I set up more lessons. I was more than a little giddy. The Big Scary Goal was not going to be impossible, and by God, I was not going to give up. I was investing in the process, in more ways than one, and the objective third-party assistance was just what I needed to set the wheels in motion.

Scribble:

- If you've ever accepted help with a challenge (whether it was organizing or pole vaulting or high school algebra), was there one small shift that made a difference?
- What might you notice if you took a closer look at your own systems and barriers?
- If you make a slight shift in your environment that leads to progress, what happens next?

CHAPTER 5

I Think I'm Getting It, But . . .

The Story: Gina

I was on the phone with a coaching client I'd been working with for about six months. Gina was a sales manager who had the advantage—or perhaps in her case, disadvantage—of working from home. Working from home for a disorganized person can either be the best thing ever, because they have an opportunity to create their own environment, or a complete recipe for disaster for the same reason. Unless there is a dedicated space for the job, which hopefully isn't the kitchen table or living room couch, work items end up scattered. Without a serious plan of action for office hours and boundaries, the temptations of running a load or five of laundry, watching TV, checking a smartphone or social media, running errands, or allowing others to visit can completely derail the day.

These were the challenges that Gina faced. She was casual about her work environment and acquisition in general. If she bought one new notebook for work-related lists and notes, she might as well buy six and use up those office supply store points. If she purchased books and never read them, or even got them out of the bags and onto the shelves, it wasn't something she stressed out about. When we started working together, Gina shared that the piles of paperwork and notes, both personal and professional, that covered most of her desk surface never even phased her. That is, until she missed online meetings due to writing things down on paper that she never looked at again, or forgot the deadline for developing a training plan for employees on their new software implementation. When these kinds of issues began to accelerate, and the boss started noticing, she reached out for help.

Sales manager Gina had recently turned a corner with her organization, but when she first took her work life back into her home she couldn't decide on a room or space. She would settle in one area, only to question it and move everything. Gina ran a little internal dialog that went something like: "OK, this corner of the main room is perfect! I love the natural light from that bay window. Although, seeing all of the cars and delivery trucks go by *is* a little distracting. Maybe I should move to the spare bedroom! That's it! I can easily fit a desk on this side if I move the dresser out of here. Oh, but then where will my dresser go? Or should I dump everything out of that and use it for my files? But file folders don't really fit. Maybe I should try . . . this oversized walk-in closet! Yes! I've heard of people using closets for office spaces. I'll just rip out the clothing bar and install a desk unit. However, that doesn't give me much room to spread paperwork out.

And it's kind of dark in there. Maybe I should just suck it up and go back to the hour-and-ten-minute commute each way." And so on.

After trying different spaces and never discovering the perfect one, Gina ended up pulling a card table into her bedroom and trying to make the best of it there. This arrangement led to a lot of disarray and a tendency to work at all hours since the computer and company phone were in her constant line of sight. To make matters worse, she would often pull her laptop down to the kitchen to check her email first thing in the morning and then never leave. Notes and paperwork ended up in both spots. When she didn't feel like heading downstairs or upstairs to look for whatever she needed, she would put off the task in question. You can see how this scenario spiraled into a semi-chaotic ambivalence towards work productivity.

When I arrived for the first time, we took a quick tour of her condo and identified a completely unutilized L-shaped loft area on the second floor for her office. Surprisingly, it was the only space in her entire home she hadn't yet tested out. It was an odd spot, but it turned out to be perfect. Since she was committed to making the telecommute work, she invested in having a half-wall built to give both a physical and mental boundary to work, and a skylight installed to help keep her alert even on dreary days. She had a decent desk, chair, and cabinet setup that we reconfigured to match her work style and aesthetic taste. We hung her favorite paintings from a local artist across from her desk, and she kept some key pieces from her collection of vintage lunch boxes out too. Her cat even had his own pillow.

We cleared out all obsolete files, outdated books, and excess supplies. To maintain the clear surfaces, Gina cut back on unnecessary purchases and started keeping her notes and lists in an online app. We transitioned from the physical organizing into weekly coaching calls over the phone when it became clear that she was keeping up with her stuff, and different issues related to managing time and tasks needed attention. Coaching was a good fit for Gina since she really liked to examine her motivations and habits and was very open to the idea of figuring out her own best solutions.

In one particular call, we reviewed her progress. Gina had implemented a routine of planning, looking at the calendar, and then setting her priorities first thing each morning. She moved into reviewing email but set a time limit to keep herself from going down unproductive rabbit holes. These new productivity habits had been so helpful in improving her efficiency and focus that she'd recently gotten a promotion. She was even mentoring another newer salesperson at the office. Her voice expressed new confidence, and she spoke routinely now about keeping her sales numbers in order and managing projects without dropping so many balls. Her space wasn't always picture-perfect, but she was seeing outcomes that made a difference in her life and increased her motivation to stay on top of everything.

I was thinking to myself about how Gina was pretty much finished with what she set out to accomplish and how our work together was coming to a close. I told her I was so impressed with everything she'd done. She had been a model client, and I lucked out in being able to work with her. We laughed about a recent story she shared—how she had pushed back with a colleague who tried to blame her for a missing sales report, how she knew it wasn't her issue because she'd kept a record of when it was turned in. It had been easy, prior to her progress, for others to shift blame to her for dropping balls, but this time was different; the missing report was on her coworker's desk under a pile of files, not her's. She stood her ground and suggested that perhaps her colleague should consider hiring some help for their office mess.

But right after the laughter died down, her voice dropped to a whisper. "But here's what I really want to talk about—what if something happens and the routine just, you know, *stops*? What if I start messing things up again? What if I'm kidding myself?" What if she was tired and blew off her planning one morning, or became sick and stayed in bed, or took a vacation and the new patterns got out of balance? All of this planning and prioritizing stuff was still very new in Gina's world, and she had a legitimate concern that her systems weren't yet second nature. She had tried other methods before, but they hadn't stuck.

It can be unsettling to suddenly be succeeding at something you previously couldn't imagine doing. When Gina started her organizing journey months before, she had not experienced much success in creating sustainable systems for herself. Now her Big Scary Goal was coming together, and she felt like she was different. Or was she? Wasn't she really just the same person who routinely didn't know how to follow a plan, much less make one? What was going to keep her moving forward? Was she just going to disappoint herself?

You may have felt this way before, too, after reaching the midpoint of a Big Scary Goal. It's like taking three steps forward, two steps back. Just when it all starts rocking along, something might trigger an old pattern or cause you to skip a key step or give into complacency. It's normal. But does it spell the end of your aspirations?

As Gina talked through her fears, I took a few moments to remind her of where she came from on her journey. She still had some old pictures of what her office used to look like. She looked back at notes from our first few calls. Whatever came next, she couldn't deny her progress. If she had done it once, wasn't it just like riding a bike? You never forget!

The Subplot: I Don't Get Always Get Angry, but When I Do . . .

KJ and I had ridden together about six times over many months when we took things up a notch. Lessons were going well. It hadn't all been as consistent as I had planned, but I was now able to get on and push off without my heart jumping straight up into my throat.

We graduated from that first parking lot to a local greenway, and I'd ridden both on my own and with Jeff numerous times in between. On one particular ride, I decided to show her a route we had tried that started on the path and progressed up into a neighborhood with some decent hills and not a ton of traffic.

It was midmorning on a weekday. Cars backed out of driveways. I stayed cool. Lawn-mowing trailers passed us. I was totally cool. A little dog came out and barked at us, threatening certain peril should we get near its territory. I became skittish, but I kept moving, and it was cool. We were riding side by side, but KJ dropped back behind when we could hear a vehicle approaching. A huge pickup truck came up alongside of us and then dropped back again. Big Truck slowed down right behind us, started honking, and then roared around us, gunning its unmuffled engine. This time I did not remain cool—I was ticked off.

I don't recall the exact words I started yelling, but I did yell, loudly, to no one in particular. There may or may not have been expletives involved, and some commentary on compensating for certain shortcomings. Big Truck didn't seem to care as he sped off to whatever deeply important and meaningful destination he had to get to, but I was sufficiently distracted enough by my anger to not be fearful of my bike.

KJ was pleased with this development—not so much my riding, but my emotion. I'd gone from being a quivering heap of a mess around vehicles to a cyclist confident enough to claim my space on the road. I have found anger to be helpful at times in the evolution of more than one Big Scary Goal. A temporary diversion from fear and a force useful to protect myself (or what I imagined needed protecting), the anger gave me a little boost. The boost lasted just long enough to see that I was making progress, which in turn led to a snippet of confidence that hadn't existed before.

This confidence even led to seeing more benefits from riding a bike—things beyond my goal that I hadn't considered at first. Being able to ride, chat with someone, and actually enjoy it wasn't originally part of the deal. Maybe I figured somewhere along the way I would appreciate some things, but what those things were exactly had not been defined.

Along with my progress, it began to crystallize that signing up for an organized ride could really be a thing that I could manage. Originally it had seemed so unattainable. At the same time, doubts would still roll in like a reliable ocean tide, then head back out once I made a step forward, then roll back in, and so on. As soon as I started to choose a ride and sign up, I would back away and start questioning myself. What if I stopped getting out for practice rides? What if one morning I just rolled over and gave up? I still wasn't fearless, and it still didn't feel natural or easy. I wondered if it never would.

During a later conversation, KJ reminded me of where I started: riding around tennis balls in a parking lot, making only left turns. Now I was on actual roads, getting pissed off when necessary, making actual headway. I had forgotten all about those early lessons. I guess my awareness of my progress hadn't sunk in, until she pointed out that I was indeed inching along the timeline I had set for myself.

To this day, I don't think I could pinpoint exactly what kept me going. I'd like to, because I would be able to give you a better idea of how to do it yourself, but I can only relate what my experience was. I suppose I recognized that a little forward motion is better than none, and that I sure didn't have a whole lot to lose. I wasn't setting out to do something that would change the world, so if it all went to hell, no harm, no foul. Getting angry was a nice little toehold on the mountain I was climbing, another exciting little shift.

Scribble:

- What has progress been like with your Big Scary Goal? Have you experienced backsliding? Back and forth?
- Where do you overlook, forget, or minimize your progress?
- What emotions have you noticed in the process?

CHAPTER 6

A Long, Slow Break

The Story: Willard

Life gets in the way sometimes. Have you ever gotten really excited about the possibility of a new change or idea only to be rudely slapped back into reality? Have you gotten really confident about a job only to be laid off when the company is bought out? Jumped into a weight loss plan and gained ten pounds? Been excited to organize a space only to pull everything out of a closet, get totally overwhelmed, and stop and leave everything sitting out for the next six weeks? What can you do to move beyond the combination of disgust and deep disappointment?

There are plenty of great reasons for a complete halt to progress with a Big Scary Goal. Some might be huge like an illness or death. Some may be as simple, but still unsettling, as a new boss. You can't handle everything that happens all at one time, despite what the rest of the world appears to expect. One of the most difficult things to handle is your assumptions—about what others can do, what others expect of you, and what you should be able to do.

Willard, known as Will, had a young family: a wife, three children under the age of eight, two cats, a dog, a hamster, and four fish. They all, except for perhaps the fish, had lots of interests and activities—hockey, gardening, camping, weightlifting, knitting, agility training, ballet—that encouraged accumulation. This crew came with lots of equipment. Everyone was on the go, all the time, and no one thought twice about dumping the detritus from their latest extracurricular adventure by the back door in the garage. Will normally rolled with all of the clutter pretty easily, but he had started to wonder if maybe he should be setting a better example. He had made some halting progress with some cabinets and drawers, pulling out stuff and rearranging it back in, but nothing ever really seemed to go together quite the way he had envisioned.

Not having had much of a model of an organized household as a kid, when Will discovered that professional organizers existed, he was all in. It was so exciting for him to realize there were real, trained people who would come to your house and get all of the clutter under control. What a genius business concept! Hiring someone to teach him organizing skills was sure to get him on track and make everything all better, he thought. After all, he had tackled everything from his advanced degree in philosophy to French cooking classes with the same enthusiasm. Why should organizing his home be any different?

When Will started his organizing sessions, he was high on the whole idea. Lots of other people do this, right? He was so eager to up his game that he scheduled an entire daylong session with the organizer he contacted. This time was going to be different than all of his previous attempts, and he was going to get it all done, no excuses. They started by tackling his packed garage, which he hoped would result in being able to park both cars inside, creating an area for his workout equipment and maybe even a small bar for entertaining with the neighbors.

It was a tall order, due in no small part to his parents keeping pretty much every aspect of his childhood in boxes and bins, which they proudly presented to him when he moved into the house five years ago. Will also tended to keep every memory, trophy, stuffed animal, or poster. He had lots of photos, framed and unframed, from parties and road races to pets and newborn children. The collecting apple did not fall far from its tree.

Undaunted, Will and his organizer, Cosmo, dived into the boxes and piles and made tons of progress in a fairly short time period. Willard's decision-making process fell into place quickly: "Yes, we can get rid of that, and that ... and especially *that*!" Soon he and Cosmo were loading up both of their vehicles with donations and recycling to haul away.

Despite his unbridled enthusiasm, Will was realistic in his expectations and knew they wouldn't be able to finish in a day. After all, how do you reset the whole garage, and the lifetime of patterns that led to its bloated condition, in just six hours? Will asked for homework and Cosmo happily complied. He continued to sort and purge all on his own after that first session, because his momentum was still high. Seeing areas of the floor that hadn't been visible since he moved in was motivating. He even scheduled four additional organizing sessions to get the whole thing under control—and maybe even add another project into the mix. Whenever he could, he would employ the guidelines he learned to tackle a spare drawer, some files in the home office, or a pile of clothes in the bedroom corner. Sometimes he texted pictures of his efforts to Cosmo, which kept him engaged and pleased with his progress. Cosmo was always decent about responding in an encouraging way. Will's wife and kids were impressed, and even pitched in between dance lessons and volunteering at the animal shelter. With all that support, and his new knowledge, he thought he might shock his family by reorganizing the whole house! He was unstoppable.

Then disaster struck. Two days prior to the next organizing session, Will tripped on a dog leash that one of the kids left on the back steps, crashed, broke his tibia, and understandably had to postpone. Cosmo was sympathetic to the situation—he sent a card and hoped the leg healed well and quickly. This kind of thing happened. They would pick up where they left off as soon as Will was all healed up.

Not long after the broken leg incident, Willard received the sobering news that his company was relocating and he needed to decide whether or not to move his family to another state. Everything was put on hold, and the company relocation process dragged on for weeks without clear resolution. He asked Cosmo if they could hold off indefinitely. Given the circumstances, Cosmo understood and agreed. And eventually Will sort of forgot how important that garage cleanup and resulting organizational know-how was. Or maybe it was not at all forgotten, but in the scheme of things it just couldn't be a relevant piece of the puzzle.

Will decided to give himself a short break from the purging and sorting—for the time being, he told himself. His leg healed slowly, and rather than uproot the whole family, he decided to separate from his company and look for a new job. The search ended up lasting about six months, a time during which he had more freedom but somehow just couldn't get up the motivation to return to the garage, or to any other space.

The organizing honeymoon excitement was gone. Will would occasionally wander out to the garage and make a feeble attempt at going through another box. He should be able to tackle this, he thought, because it seemed everyone else could. His neighbor's garage across the street mocked him with its epoxy floor, pegboard with tools, and shelves full of matching bins. They didn't have any issues with organizing at all. It was so easy for them.

As if to add insult to injury, his mom brought over all of his old concert T-shirts from the nineties, three bins full. Thanks, Mom. She reasoned that if he was interested in organizing, he ought to have all of his stuff—and should have more room to store things now. The bins were dutifully placed next to several donation bags that he and Cosmo hadn't been able to fit in either vehicle the day of the big purge—eight months earlier. He stared disconsolately around the garage. One car fit. Two did not. It was all over.

When it rains, it pours, right? You're rocking along, and then your grown child moves back in, the dog dies, or the refrigerator blows out while you're out of town—or all three. Sometimes it's just not a good time to try to fit another big change, no matter how positive, into the schedule. It's totally understandable and acceptable. But then there's the problem of inertia. How do you break out of it to get back to that good motivating place? What does it take?

After Will slipped into a groove with his new job, things did settle back down—at least as far as anything ever settled down with his family. One weekend afternoon when his family was out shopping for martial arts equipment and the house was quiet, he decided on a whim to clear out the kitchen junk drawer. Dumping out the contents, a business card fluttered to the floor. He reached down to pick it up, turned it over, and saw that it was Cosmo's. Maybe it was time to send him a text.

The Subplot: My Long, Slow Brake

I don't recall exactly how we got off track. It may have been around the time my father started getting really sick, or when my mother-in-law started getting really sick, or when Jeff started traveling for work almost nonstop. I don't know. I just know that the weeks were ticking by, and Flo did not make it out of the garage with me. I was canceling and postponing my lessons with KJ. Then the habit went out of me, and I felt defeated because no long ride was happening. It was just further and further out of reach.

Not only was the ride out of reach, but writing this book seemed like a total pipe dream. At this point, the connection between the ride and the book was now firmly established, and the two goals together had created a nice double accountability situation. I had felt that initial high of excitement about possibilities and was now looking back at the lost time with some resignation and an internal "I-told-you-so" voice berating me. What was I thinking, anyway? Who was I to attempt such a thing?

Dealing with my father's hospital and rehab care, moving him into assisted living, and getting his home on the market were all monumental tasks due to my having to travel almost two hours each way to get to him. He was grumpy and resentful, and I felt horribly guilty, but certain things had to be addressed. Furniture had to be divided up, sold, or given away. Discussions with lots of doctors, and then between family members, had to take place. After so many decisions, I would need to return home and shuttle my kids to whatever activities they needed to attend, handle the dogs, see clients, do life.

My situation certainly wasn't unique. I have plenty of friends, family, and clients who have to take on extra family responsibilities while their own kids are still growing up. But it seemed that no sooner did we get my father situated and on a slightly healthier track than my mother-in-law began losing her cancer battle. Then my father ended up in the hospital yet again. October through December of 2016 was a sad, disorienting blur. We lost both of them in rapid succession, and our family headed into the holidays with heavy hearts and a new family dynamic to become accustomed to. We had to make time to grieve, and I just wasn't feeling the bike-book thing anymore. I was bored with myself for even considering it. I started to assume that the idea was cracked from the very start.

This situation is the sort of juncture of action versus inaction at which many settle into complacency, like Willard. I guess my only saving grace was that although I wasn't physically hopping on Flo and taking off, the idea of riding was still pinballing around in the back of my mind. Because the goal was always tied to this book, and because deep down I would be forever disgusted with myself for giving up, I kept internally processing my options.

Even if tons of time had already flown by, there was still an opportunity to try again. I mean, the human race has built pyramids, explored space, climbed Everest. Was my little challenge such a big, hairy deal? I still had that glimmer of the original inspiration, so the question changed from "What was I thinking?" to "What if I just cut my losses and start over?" Maybe I could just clear the decks and pretend that the first go-round really didn't even happen.

Yet more time ticked away. The year 2017 dawned, and before I knew it, spring arrived. In May of that year, our family made the decision to downsize and simplify by moving to a different home over the summer, and my extended grieving process started to, ever so slightly, loosen its grip. I got very buzzed, anticipating all of the project management aspects of moving—I kind of like moving—and organizing our new spaces was healing for me. The last time I had moved into a new home, I was not a professional organizer, and I had two very small children. Now I had several years of experience, and the kids were much older and independent. This move was an amazing, and a conveniently distracting, opportunity.

Several weeks after we settled in at the new house, Flo hung dejectedly from her newly installed bike rack in the new garage, looking at me reproachfully whenever I came and went.

> Flo: "Hey, *there* she is! Hey, it's sunny and seventy degrees! I'd like to get out of here for a little bit?"
>
> Me: "I know, I know. But I'm on my way to a client. Maybe tomorrow."
>
> Flo: "I've heard that before. It's like you don't like me anymore. I'm not built to hang out here and catch dust."

Me, ashamed: "Of course I like you. Although I'm also still secretly, completely intimidated by you. Maybe I wasn't the right owner for you."

Flo: "Girl, I am not a puppy. I don't require feeding, training, letting out in the backyard. I'll admit I'm not furry, but I think I could be Insta-worthy. Come *on*! You were doing so well!"

Yes, I talked to her sometimes. Still do. I don't know if objects have personalities, but I do think they have energies. One day Flo's energy, for whatever reason, started getting through to me.

After the months of inactivity, I hesitantly considered reaching back out to KJ for a refresher lesson. Time to begin all over, once again.

> **Scribble:**
>
> - Think back over some prior life transitions. What do you remember about your productivity during those transitions?
> - When have you lost your balance and decided to just go with it?
> - What sorts of messages or energies can you pick up from your surroundings?

CHAPTER 7

Back in the Saddle

The Story: Nicole

Nicole was a two-year survivor of breast cancer. Normally organized and on top of her game, her diagnosis and treatment pulled her attention away from her routine practices of decluttering, ordering, and planning. She wasn't a neat freak or anything, but keeping things straight and accessible in her three-bedroom bungalow was important to her. Prior to the disruption, she had maintained a close relationship with her label maker and felt tremendous satisfaction when she looked into her closets and could see exactly where everything should go. She grew up in a military family, too, so embracing discipline and streamlined living were branded into her psyche.

Nicole had never been too attached to things or been much of a shopper, at least for clothing or books or other items people seemed to hang onto. She appreciated and recognized that the organization she already had in place at home served her well throughout her health challenge. Not having a lot of excess stuff to deal with meant that she could focus her attention on the things she needed to do to recover and heal. The worst stresses, aside from recuperating from surgery and getting used to a new normal, involved dealing with her rescue pets—two dachshund mixes, one with three legs, and an elderly, cross-eyed Siamese.

Her adult daughter, Cody, lived nearby. Cody was a huge support to Nicole in tracking the myriad follow-up appointments, staying on top of the pet care, and even creating a binder for Nicole with divisions for insurance statements, post-op instructions, questions, articles, nutrition information, and more. Although other medical paperwork and mail had piled up, and Nicole hadn't gone through her clothing in ages to weed out things that no longer suited her, there had been a baseline of order throughout the treatment process.

Or had there? Actually, quite a few things hadn't been getting her attention. In the twelve months since being given a clean bill of health, she hadn't felt like dealing with any of her stuff anymore—physical or mental. Cody noticed that Nicole seemed to have more trouble remembering and managing small details that never used to give her issues, like using her planner or checking on her online bill pay accounts. Despite regaining her balance health-wise, the organizing scale was beginning to tip toward some low-level chaos, or maybe mid-level chaos. Nicole was exhausted, too, and felt like a different person with different priorities. Who gives a flip about matching hangers or printed file labels when you've managed to cheat death?

Taken out of her regular habit and routine, Nicole had zero interest in decluttering her spaces, and it was showing. She would rather head out to enjoy a little mindless garage sale hopping or catch a movie with a friend than go through mail or put the Halloween decorations away. The house had small stacks popping up in every room now, from new pet toys and food in the laundry area to online orders, still in boxes, in the spare bedroom. Cody felt some alarm each time she walked in to find the formerly neat living room increasingly covered in magazines, bags of dollar-store purchases, and scrapbooking supplies—her mom's one indulgent hobby—but she chose not to mention it. What good would it do to harass Nicole about the state of the house when she was just grateful to have her around?

You may have heard of the term situational disorganization—the sort of chaos of time and space that occurs following significant life events. Stressful events, whether they are perceived as positive or negative, disrupt natural rhythms and take our attention away from familiar routines. Often, although not always, they are unexpected, so you don't have any prep time, or ability, to think ahead. It's not that you don't understand how to organize or maintain order, it's just that you simply can't—at least for a time. Like Nicole, you may even find that the situation has fundamentally changed who you are—physically, mentally, or spiritually. The tricky part is, in order to get back to some sort of organizing equilibrium, you have to take the new normal into account. Organizing systems that worked before the baby came, or the parent died, or you changed careers, will likely no longer serve you the way they used to. It's like switching from automatic to manual transmission in a car: you're going to grind a few gears before you figure out how to move forward.

You also may not even be aware of when or how much this disorder sneaks up on you. In my experience, it only takes a little out-of-the-ordinary instance to snap you back to attention.

One morning Nicole climbed out of bed, instinctively stepped over a pile of shoes, navigated the box-and-bag obstacle course to her bathroom, and opened up the medicine cabinet to pull out a prescription. She jumped back, startled, when little amber-colored plastic bottles, boxes of Band-Aids, and other supplies came tumbling out everywhere, all over the counter and the floor. Picking a bottle up, she noted that it was six months out of date—and was actually for the cat.

Nicole suddenly had a flash of insight. Scanning the room at the state of affairs, it was like she was really seeing her surroundings for the first time in months. "What is all of this junk?" she wondered. Why had she allowed a pile of clean, but unfolded, towels to end up on the floor? Opening up the cabinet under the sink, she gasped as she recognized it was totally stuffed, and she had no idea what was in it beyond the first few bottles of shampoo and the industrial-sized body lotion in the front row. Walking through other rooms, she felt the same dismay and disgust. It was like an alien from Planet Clutter had been covertly camping out in the attic, emerging at night to gleefully throw crap around and then cram it all back into cabinets and drawers.

What had happened? Cancer happened, for one thing, so certainly the situation had dictated some different priorities. Nicole was discouraged by the jumbled state of her formerly clear and calm space, and she also remembered that for the first time since before Cody was born, she had let some bills slide past their due dates and ended up paying late fees. She recalled missing a family birthday party because she double-booked it with a trip out of town. She started recounting all of her missteps to herself: dumping things when she came through the back door, mindlessly making small purchases here and there, skipping meal planning, ignoring paperwork. All understandable, and hopefully forgivable, but certainly uncomfortable. The awareness of all of this disorder was creeping up on her, and maybe the camping alien wasn't so benign.

If she didn't get smart and start working her way back, her surroundings were eventually going to get her into more trouble with herself. The situation called for some deep breathing and some acceptance of where she was. Beating herself up about the state of affairs and her new awareness of it wasn't going to get any of the stuff under control. She would never chastise a friend for dropping balls after a large-scale life event, so why berate herself for the same situation? With more self-compassion and acceptance, what was possible?

She wasn't as sharp on managing lots of details, but she could start making some better lists. She didn't have the same old enthusiasm for ironing and folding, but maybe if she cut back on her impulse shopping she wouldn't have so much of that to worry about.

Nicole took a few minutes to have her coffee, collect her thoughts, and call Cody. She asked her when her first available Saturday was and if maybe, just maybe, she could see her way to helping out just a bit more—this time with some intentionality around clearing out the excess that had accumulated. Setting a date, and promising to take themselves out to dinner afterward, they agreed to work together on the countertop piles and at least one overstuffed closet. Cody was thrilled to help and relieved that her mother had the beginning of a plan and some motivation. Although Nicole had plenty of regrets over letting it all get out of whack, she was relieved too. It didn't matter what had already happened; she couldn't do anything about that anyway. She had a hunch that it was going to require several Saturdays and several dinners, but together, they could tackle it one step at a time.

The Subplot: Substitutions, Stalls, and Toes in the Water

When we last left off, I was a weakling again, which for me is a comfortable and familiar state of being. As I described in the last chapter, during the whole spring and summer of 2017, I had been canceling bike lessons right and left, my excuse generally involving that pet project: the sale of the first house and the move into the other. This downsizing thing was a handy story to use. There were other philosophical reasons for the move, but a lot of it was about walking my talk in terms of consumption and a smart use of space. On another level, it gave me some great rationalizations for stalling: I have to get ready for an open house; I have to wait for the thrift store to do a pickup; I'm meeting with house painters, etc. I was also in the thick of my coaching training, working with clients, and being a mom. Busy was the badge of honor I secretly hated but kept up in order to avoid thinking about what wasn't happening.

I was more than ready and willing to give up on riding, to move on. I hadn't told anyone other than Jeff and KJ that I was thinking about this whole bike-book thing, so there was absolutely no need to be too terribly embarrassed or uptight. We all have big ideas we don't follow through on. There are more natural ways to prove yourself to yourself. I felt a mix of relief and self-recrimination when I postponed the rides, but it was so much easier to put pressure on myself in other areas. The planning and moving tasks are fun, and second nature for me: Meet with the realtor. Take the dogs to daycare during house showings. Check on the garage shelving installation. Organize and pack. Purge and declutter!

All of the work and planning dulled some of that extreme grief I had been experiencing, which was the real cause of the disruption of my goal. There's nothing like a massive, life-altering project to protect me from processing pain and disappointment.

    I hadn't even been pretending to do any sort of workout routine. Looking back on my calendar, I realize now that I had done a slick job of lulling myself into complacency. The journey had been taking much longer than I wanted anyway, and I certainly hadn't been in love with all of the process. Engaging in an uncomfortable, fear-inspiring activity with a distinct possibility of complete failure attached wasn't easy. I don't have the baseline athletic ability parallel to our chapter heroine Nicole's baseline organizing ability, so between that, the grief, and the house move there were three strikes against me. I had allowed, perhaps even invited, a situation to keep me from balancing my chosen priorities. When I stopped to consider what I'd been doing, I felt uncomfortable exasperation with myself. Dropping this particular goal was a disappointment of my own creation. I went down a bit of a dark hole, beating myself up for not following through.

    The idea was still in me, of course, because here we are. When I considered contacting KJ, I thought long and hard about whether or not it was the right time to begin again, what with all of my other commitments. I am not only a professional organizer but also a professional rationalizer. More than once I started to pump the tires and get back on but froze cold as soon as I walked into the garage. I was scared and intimidated once again. And adding the ride back into the current goals might screw up the balance I was so consciously and carefully creating, right?

I have never been comfortable with the concept of treating myself kindly, which is ironic since I advise it for clients all the time. When I've tested out self-compassion exercises or guided meditations, I have had an extremely difficult time settling in. It feels squishy and unstructured, like I'm not holding myself to an appropriate standard. My ego says, "What, you mean I just pat myself on the back and say, 'there, there, poor thing,' whenever I screw something up? Where's the improvement in that?" If I take time to dig a little deeper, perhaps self-compassion means I have to acknowledge something like an emotion, which is yucky. I continue working with my challenges with self-compassion to this day. But all that said, I did test out some lighter ways of assessing the situation, mostly in the form of:

- Didn't I have a little bit of fun riding that bike?
- Wouldn't I like to have some fun again?
- What in the world do I have to lose at this point?

I did, of course, finally reach back out to KJ. Fifty miles on my fiftieth birthday was a long-gone opportunity, so there went that perfect, poetic idea. But one morning I decided to just send her a quick "Hi, how are you doing?" Nothing too committal. I casually put it out there that I had been researching cycling events online again—researching is another great way for me to procrastinate and imagine I'm actually doing something. Naturally, KJ being KJ, she responded almost instantly. "What distance are you looking at?" she asked.

So, she actually read it. And responded. "Distance?" Honestly, I had no idea what distance I was looking at. I didn't even know what I was doing by reaching back out, and the whole concept felt foggy and disjointed. Maybe it was my version of a midlife crisis. I don't know, was it crazy to think I was missing the progress I had made, even though I was almost back at square one again? One short email had made all the difference, and we set up our next lesson. Time to jump back in.

Scribble:

- What's your current situation with that Big Scary Goal?
- What are you, or might you be, waiting for?
- What needs to happen next?

CHAPTER 8

Experimentation

The Story: Karl

Karl was a sixty-ish, newly retired executive, gearing up to tackle a lot of old stuff tucked away in closets and the spare bedroom. He wanted to turn this room from a dumping ground into an artistic, creative space designed specifically for his interests. So did his wife, because he was driving her a little crazy. He was somewhat of a Renaissance man, dabbling in painting, woodworking, writing, music, and genealogy, but the sudden shift into having a lot of time on his hands threw him into a tailspin of puttering around the house and leaving his hobby accoutrements behind him wherever he went. The room in question was not fit to contain him, and it contained boxes from his old office, gift wrapping supplies, files from forty years of marriage and family life, books and more books, pictures yet to be hung, and his vinyl record collection.

He knew that the spare bedroom needed serious attention, but the prospect of going through everything seemed confusing and off-putting. Where to start? He had recently binge-watched a show on home organization, and he wanted to give the ideas he had seen a shot. He even put organizing time in on his calendar at regular intervals and headed out to the store for bins and boxes. He figured he needed to have supplies on hand, and the boxes surely would do the trick in disguising whatever it was he wanted to keep around. He hadn't decided exactly what those things were, of course.

Despite loving the freedom of not having to go into an office every day, the sudden lack of structure came with a dark side—an ever-dwindling lack of motivation for culling and categorizing. Karl took about a month after his last days in the office to relax and do a little traveling, and then he made his lofty bedroom-makeover plans. Now there was nothing but open time stretching ahead.

Making an effort to get going on these plans seemed to go to the wayside pretty much as soon as he woke up, made coffee, and turned on the news. News would turn into talk shows; talk shows would turn into getting hooked on a historical series; lunch may or may not have happened. When he finally managed to turn the TV off, Karl occasionally wandered into the spare bedroom to gaze at the stacks and piles. Then he would calmly turn around and walk back out in search of a happier distraction. Trimming the bonsais, perhaps.

Before Karl knew it, the days sped past, and he had taken no steps toward his goal. He never realized, or perhaps never admitted, that during his working life he might have had issues with goal-setting, planning, and organization. He had assistants who tackled most of his scheduling and administrative tasks. He felt defeated and self-conscious. Feeling defeated and self-conscious led to feeling confused about where to begin, and feeling confused led to no action. If he didn't even try, then he didn't have to face the idea that maybe he was not naturally very good at keeping things in order. He could blame laziness, or he could just convince himself that if he wanted to, he could get that room in order any old time. Now was just not that time.

It's not that Karl didn't want a nice space for himself. He desperately wanted it. He craved an area that felt peaceful and controlled, an area that felt uniquely suited to him and the things he had always planned to do when retirement came along. However, when he walked through the door of the "landfill," as he called it, insecurity took over. Not being accustomed to indecisiveness, and especially about such trivial things as books and papers, Karl's feelings were uncomfortable and mentally taxing. The room had become like a sentient organism, deriding him for his avoidance. He also had mixed feelings about putting in the amount of work he suspected the project would take. He just retired, after all. Wasn't he supposed to be taking it easy? Why should he spend all of this hard-won free time clearing out junk? His wife had, for the time being, decided to stay out of the whole situation: she just shut the door.

All that said, Karl ventured into the room one day in a fit of inspiration, ready to do a little work. His wife had left for her book club meeting, so he was free to try some things without feeling like she was watching. Maybe just a few minutes wouldn't be so bad, he thought. He mentally took some pressure off—it already looked like a scene from a horror film in there, and he could not possibly make it any worse—and just decided to see what might happen if he started. He looked around and finally figured it didn't matter which area he began with. How about the southwest corner where those boxes from his old office came to rest?

He reviewed one more organizing video online, set a timer for one hour, cranked up a little Stravinsky on the turntable, and began making some progress with separating books and papers. "Just tackle one category," the guest organizing expert on the morning show suggested the other day. "Put like with like." He could do that at least. He pushed back the thoughts on how he should be able to do it quicker, with more conviction, or with more aesthetic style.

He considered his paperwork, and he categorized or discarded what he found. He even hummed a little, getting into a groove with his sorting. The few things that actually made it into a file drawer several years back were not even close to being relevant anymore—gas bills from 1997, a manual for the vacuum that conked out three years ago—so into the recycling pile they went. This organizing business wasn't so scary after all.

Even though much of what he had read and seen suggested color-coding files, he never really paid attention to color, nor did he remember to buy colored folders. What if he didn't even need files? What if, after purging most of the last ten or so years of paperwork, all he needed was a couple of shallow trays with stacks on a shelf? Then he could use the oversized file drawers to tuck away the vinyl collection that had been stuck between those two armchairs, one of which was going to the thrift store anyway. Killing two birds! The whole idea was suddenly an exciting proposition. Pieces of the puzzle were starting to fall into place.

The timer went off. Stepping back to examine his handiwork, Karl realized he would actually like to continue the job. Who would have thought? He sat back down, pulled a box of office supplies over, and . . .

The Subplot: It Doesn't Matter How It Happens

The riding lessons resumed, and it seemed I wasn't set back by my folly as far as I had feared. Flo was content again and quit berating me. KJ let me know she was going out of town for a bit, and that I should ride a route I'd mapped out on my own before she returned. I had mixed feelings about this proposition, not so much because I thought I couldn't do it, although fear of the unknown did creep in from time to time, but more because it seemed like effort. I would have to pick a morning, get up early, make sure I had stuff to wear ready, fill a water bottle, get the bike rack out and hooked up, drive to the route, get out, and do it. Then I would have to drive back, reverse the process, and shower, all before I start meeting with clients. Like I said—effort.

Somehow, these efforts didn't seem so daunting when I had to meet another person, or at least when I felt more determined to follow through with the plan. External motivators are super helpful but aren't always practical. None of what was being asked of me was particularly difficult—I'm the one who came up with this whole nonsensical idea. So what was the deal?

Perhaps there comes a point where we have to admit to ourselves that despite verbally committing to a goal, despite investing in resources, and despite taking some steps to achieve it, we can still feel sort of "meh" about the whole thing. Maybe we get bored, or try to talk ourselves out of it when it seems like a hassle. In the moment, it's easier to roll over and quit or delay than to think we have a right to be improving upon something uncomfortable or different. Then it's easier to blame ourselves and revert to saying, "I'm just not cut out for this," or, "I'm too lazy," or even, "I'm accepting my limitations and I'm OK with them." It's hard to envision doing difficult things our own way, or a way that's different from what an expert prescribes. But until we learn some basics from experience, how do we even figure out what works?

It's sort of like learning to cook. Initially, it's best to follow some standard recipes, even if they feel constricting or rigid, before you start creating your own. I was reminded of this watching a ridiculous cooking reality show where one of the contestants—we'll call him Steve—steadfastly refused to follow any of the given instructions: "I always do my own thing and put my own special 'Steve' stamp on my cooking." Despite his impressive confidence, he knew almost nothing about how to cook. What resulted was, of course, a literal hot mess. And his team lost out on $5,000 too, but hey, Steve, you be you.

Anyway, KJ also reminded me that I needed to go out at least twice a week in order to be ready for a long ride. I planned on an early Tuesday morning before I met with clients, but just about the time I started to slide into something easier—believe it or not, answering email—my client for that day canceled, and I was forced to confront the fact that I had nothing else standing in my way. I was not feeling it, but my intuition told me to get busy. I wanted to at least report in that I had done something. I saddled up Flo on the bike rack and we headed out to the greenway. I was still not brave enough to just head out directly from my house, so driving to the spot was what worked for the time being.

This particular ride was pivotal for me. It was a gorgeous day, after several disappointing early spring cold snaps, and because I was out late-morning, there were not too many people or cars. I had figured out some ways to go in and out of the greenway trail into some less-trafficked neighborhoods. Yes, a few cars. No dump trucks. I set an app that would track my time and results, and I began what turned into the most fun I've had on a bike since I was probably five or six years old.

Despite the nice weather, almost no one else was out. I didn't have to worry about anyone seeing me if I did something stupid, like fall. After about fifty minutes of just riding wherever I felt like riding, I felt confident enough to play around with things like—please don't laugh—taking my hands off the handlebars to scratch my nose or grab my water bottle, standing up when I pedaled, and not eternally riding the brakes heading downhill. I noticed that when I was trying to stand up my right leg felt particularly shaky—what was that about? What would happen if I allowed myself to go faster? What would happen if I shifted down or up, less or more?

It may sound crazy to you, but the whole ride was sort of a revelation for me. Maybe if I got out more and just messed around, then I wouldn't feel that shakiness and paralysis. I kept riding and experimenting until my timer went off then headed back to the parking lot. I think it was the first time I've ever been truly sad that a period of physical activity ended—no joke. And looking back on the ride, I wasn't fearful even once. Then again, no one was around to make me feel self-conscious either.

Experimentation can be an amazing tool if you take the time for it and pay attention. The privacy made me feel comfortable, that it was OK to screw up or look inept. As long as they didn't involve the loss of large quantities of blood, I was ready to embrace mistakes and learn from them. And thanks to the knowledge gained from the previous lessons—even those that happened over a year earlier—I had just enough experience to keep my balance.

Scribble:

- Experiment with writing, drawing, telling, or imagining an ending for Karl's story. What else did he try?
- Did he ever get the room cleared and rearranged? What did that get him?
- What sort of experiment could you conduct with your Big Scary Goal?

CHAPTER 9

The One "How-To" Chapter

> It is wise to learn to embrace with hospitality that which is awkward and difficult.
>
> —John O'Donohue, *Anam Cara: A Book of Celtic Wisdom*

After reading through the introduction, or just the first few pages, many of you may have skipped the other chapters and stopped here. That's cool. I get that some folks are thinking, "Geez-o-Pete, can't she quit talking about shame and bikes and crap and just let us know how to get organized?"

Your thoughts speak loudly—no bike story at the end of this one. In this chapter I will outline a system I created a few years back for giving clients a starting point. It was first presented in my blog and I've expanded and tweaked it as I've learned more. It works fabulously for some, who go on to apply it in other areas after the first session. For others, it's more of a starting point—perhaps forgotten after the first session but still useful in the beginning just to get the ball rolling. It covers ground that has been covered in different ways in other books and methods, but it's what I've used with clients for a long time, so it does have a fair amount of tire-kicking credibility.

I wanted to come up with a system that could function as that solid beginning for my clients, because the most common comment I get is, "I just don't know where to start." I wanted a system that came from my own viewpoint and experience but could be modified and tailored for the individual working with it. One day, out of nowhere—well, actually, in the shower—the idea for this protocol came to me as a way to give clients that initial something to grab onto. I never envisioned any of it being a book. First, it was just sticky notes on a wall next to large quantities of items stored nonsensically on shelves. Then it became a blog series, then many, many more client sessions where it seemed it actually helped. I would return to the scenes of the crimes to find that my sticky notes had been moved to another space and utilized in another way.

My clients, many who are chronically disorganized, seemed to find the process eye-opening. Quite a few had already been unknowingly working on various segments of the system, but in the wrong order, or without connecting how they could all fit together. I believe everyone has organizational instincts buried somewhere, but they often get jumbled up or discounted because they don't look or sound like the commonly held ideas of organization.

The system is pragmatic and the letters create a convenient acronym. All good systems have catchy acronyms, right? It's good for those of you who just want something to encourage some action when you're stuck. This method should help you in answering some of the eternal organizing questions: Where should I start? How do I begin? Why have other attempts not worked?

At this point, you may want to grab your own sticky notes, whatever colors you like best, and a permanent marker. Pick a disorganized space, any space. Here we go:

The LESS Method

Because utilizing LESS leads to more—more confidence, more ability, more peace, more control. There are more "mores," but we'll stop with those for now.

"L" is for Learn

If you like and need reminders, write an "L" on the first note, write the word "Learn" under it, and stick it somewhere on the wall or a surface in your chosen space.

Learn. We generally do not know what all we have until we purposefully take steps to find out. We also are often not aware of how we work best with the items and information around us. For example, "L" is about learning what exactly is in your desk drawer; it's not just office supplies but rather:

- Seven pens that work, five that don't, and two you just don't like

- Eleven stray rubber bands, six of which disintegrate when handled
- A pack of sticky notes (those will come in handy)
- A travel-size bottle of mouthwash (leaking)
- A box of mechanical pencils
- Notepads from the last hotel you stayed at, the Realtor down the street, the last conference you attended
- Five unopened boxes of paper clips
- A fork, two packets of ketchup, and a coffee stirrer
- Two CD-R discs (used, but unlabeled)
- A screwdriver
- Thirty-two business cards (not yours, and not entered into contacts)
- Seventy-six cents, and one Canadian penny
- A bottle of correction fluid with a stuck cap
- Envelopes, varying sizes
- Greeting cards, none of which fit said envelopes
- Mardi Gras beads

And so on. "Wow," you're thinking as you read this, "it's just like you're really here." I have been here—many times. You negated the volume of stuff by calling the whole drawer "office supplies," and there is way more in that drawer than you could imagine. But be honest here: until you checked you did *not* know you had a grand total of five boxes of paper clips. The point is that you really can't know at all how to begin clearing and purging until you know exactly what all hides in the space. You have to learn, or remind yourself, what you have and come to grips with it before you can progress.

What happens when you pick up some of the objects? Do you recall where they came from, how they ended up where they are? You might not. How do those objects make you feel? Was the item a purchase? A gift? Something brought home by a loved one? What's the story behind it?

Learning is also about knowing ourselves. Most of us have instincts that we regularly ignore. Maybe deep down we know we work better when the surfaces are clear. Or maybe we need to experiment with leaving things visible, so we can remember them. Try sitting in a cluttered space and really looking around. Take an empty paper towel tube and "telescope" it around the room—what do you notice? Think back to a time when the space was clearer, or maybe even empty, like when you first moved in. What sorts of things happened along the way that resulted in the current hot mess?

It's common that when I'm first talking with a client and I ask them how long the space has felt uncomfortable to them, there is a dawning realization that, "It all started when [the baby came, I lost my job, my business exploded, I learned I had diabetes, etc.]." Or maybe your spaces have always been disorganized, because of a brain difference or because you never had any organizing modeling growing up. Knowing how it all started seems to help, kind of like a diagnosis.

I think it gives a little comfort that there's at least one understandable stressor behind all of the clutter.

Knowledge is power. Here's a challenge for you: Go to the space you selected (or a small section of it) and find out what all is in it. Make a list and put a star next to the things you had forgotten about, things that surprised you, or things that still have shrink wrap or tags on them. Ask yourself, as objectively and with as little self-judgment as possible, "How did this item originate?" Think about what about you is connected to the item, and in what way. Be curious. Notice what you feel and allow yourself to feel it.

"E" is for Evaluate

If you're creating sticky notes, the next one is "E" and "Evaluate"—put it next to the "L" note.

Learning can often be enjoyable, because most of us like to learn about ourselves, and we sometimes discover that things we had misplaced, lost, or forgotten are still with us. Discovering old photographs, or a watch you'd forgotten you bought, or a stash of several hundred dollars, certainly keeps your attention.

Evaluate is probably the most critical step, because within this part of the process you start to unearth the reasons behind why you buy, save, accumulate, and put things most anywhere but where they really need to be. For that reason, it can also be the most troubling part of the process—it's why I keep tissues handy in sessions. If you've tried to get organized before, you probably know some of the questions you're supposed to ask yourself: Do I use this item? Do I love this item? Do I have space for this item?

Those are good questions to begin the process of determining, by evaluating, whether or not the things you own are relevant to your life. But I like to drill down to some other ideas, because you need to know what your clutter really means for you. Sometimes, in an organizing session, a client will get a little bit twisted around a weird object. Something that should be easy to make a decision about but for whatever reason causes a hiccup in the process. Let's go back to our list of office supplies that we learned about in the desk drawer, and let's take those Mardi Gras beads we found under the five boxes of paper clips. Let's say I pull them out and you just cannot figure out what the best way to move forward would be. Here's how the conversation might go:

> Me: "Do you use these beads for something in the office?"
>
> Imaginary You: "No."
>
> M: "Do you love them?"
>
> IY: "Well, love is kind of a strong word, but they hold great memories."
>
> M: "How did you get them?"
>
> IY: "An old boyfriend just gave them to me in college."

M: "How do you feel about that?"

IY: "Well, actually, he *was* kind of a jerk, and of course I'm happily married to someone else with two children, a dog, and a guinea pig, so . . . OK, maybe they aren't such great memories."

M: "How did they get here?"

IY: "I think I was running around picking stuff up before my mother-in-law came over. We were having her for Christmas Eve dinner, and I had already burned one set of cookies and was airing the house out when I realized I totally hadn't cleared off the dining room table and . . ."

M: "Pardon my interruption, but they got here how?"

IY: "Oh, I'm sorry, yes! Anyway . . . I grabbed them and tossed them in the desk drawer."

M: "How long ago was that?"

IY: "Maybe three years ago?"

M: "Do they make you a more successful you?"

Silence.

M: "What's the worst thing that could happen if you got rid of them?"

More silence.

IY: "I wouldn't have Mardi Gras beads in my desk drawer anymore?"

M: "And does that take away from your work here at the desk?"

IY: "No, of course not."

M: "What would you think about those beads a few weeks from now?"

IY: "I doubt I would remember them at all."

M: "So, could you pitch them?"

IY: "What?! And put them in the landfill?"

M: "OK, so what alternatives do we have?"

IY: "My sister has younger kids that would probably enjoy using them for dressing up."

M: "Good thought! Let's set them aside for her."

The beads fall into a category that I call "pivotal objects." These are the slightly off-beat, weird things that can really get us hung up in an organizing process if we don't take a little time to work through them. Pivotal objects certainly aren't always things we decide to discard, but once we figure out their value we can give them the right storage. Making decisions generally goes more smoothly after working through a pivotal object.

If you made a chart of your decision-making results with all of those things in the drawer, carefully thinking through the pros and cons of how everything shakes out, it might begin to look something like this (This is for illustrative purposes only. You don't need to make a chart):

Useful	Successful	Beautiful	Guilt-ridden	Irrelevant	Just Plain Weird
Three pens	Business cards (networking)	Nothing	Five boxes of paper clips	Pads of notepaper	Mardi Gras beads

Working through these thoughts and feelings can initially wear you out and maybe bring up some disgust or other difficult feelings, but once you get the hang of the process it moves much faster. There is such a thing as decision fatigue, and that's why it's helpful to have another, nonbiased person help during this part of organizing. Depending upon the objects, taking a break here and there helps too. It may be much easier to go through the kids' toys from four years ago than it is to go through a grandparent's years of saved paperwork, or vice versa, so plan your time and process accordingly. Feel free to express the feelings that come up during your evaluation phase—and take some comfort that whether it's skeletons in your closets, or beads in your desk drawers, we all have some strange things we're hanging onto.

The next two letters get to the meat of any organizing project: sorting and systematizing. We're on the downhill ride now, folks. You can make two more sticky notes: "S" for "Sort" and "S" for "System." All four notes together can serve as a reminder of the process.

"S" is for "Sort"

If you've learned what you have, and evaluated the usefulness, attractiveness, importance, or sentimentality of the objects you're organizing, you're ready to move on to creating the categories that are most meaningful to your situations. So next we need some of those standard sorting categories that most all organizers use, such as:

- Keep
- Pitch
- Donate
- Recycle
- Relocate

A chart for those categories might look like this (again just for illustration):

Keep	Pitch	Recycle	Relocate	Donate	Special
Three pens	Ketchup, coffee stirrers	Pads of notepaper	Fork	Five boxes of paper clips	Mardi Gras beads (give to sister)

This stage is where you sort out and collect your categories into piles or even boxes or bins. Sometimes I find that there are items that defy these categories—the aforementioned Mardi Gras beads, maybe a vintage comic book collection, barely used designer handbags, or 1920s-era family photos. If someone has a great reason for creating a new or different grouping, I'm all for it as long as it moves progress on the project *and* we create a clear plan for how the items will reach their final destination.

On the other side of the coin, numerous new categories can actually be a camouflage for the evil anti-S, "Stalling"—we do not want a sticky note for stalling. Are you thinking up so many different ways to distribute your stuff you won't ever be able to actually make good on the promises? If you're saving old cookbooks for a granddaughter who lives five hundred miles away, are they ever going to get to her, and are you *positive* she is going to appreciate them? There's nothing more disheartening than saving up a bunch of your unwanted treasure for someone and having them completely reject it, so tread carefully and monitor your feelings and opinions with regard to others.

Often the extra, finely detailed categories are a way to put off the process of letting go—ask yourself *why* everything must have the perfect landing spot before you pass it on. Is it easing the guilt you feel for spending the money in the first place and then never really using the item? Does the thought of strangers using the item bother you for some reason? Sort with clear purpose, and stick to your sort. You may also circle back to your "L" because hopefully you're getting some clarity around how to prevent all of the stuff from getting out of control in the first place—like backing off on the bargain shopping and routinely relocating items to their correct rooms. It takes as much energy to put something away as it does to drop it on the counter, especially factoring in the time you'll waste looking for it later.

You should end up with the items in piles or boxes in each category (keep, relocate, recycle, etc.), ready for action. You can label those piles with sticky notes, too, to minimize confusion. In the heat of your organizing frenzy, you don't want to discover your family passports have all been thrown into the shred pile.

Take the donations, recycling, and trash away first and *fast*—call for a pickup if you need to—to get them out of view. Or bribe a friend to do it for you. Get a little exercise by taking all of the items that belong somewhere else in the house to their approximate homes. I say approximate, recognizing that organizing has a domino effect—once you get one space cleared you may not have the ideal home for some items, which means the LESS system will eventually need to migrate to other spaces. Eventually. Don't get too caught up in the runaround and distraction of other disorganized areas. Let's finish this space up first by moving on to the last letter.

"S" is for System

The last step—creating a system—is the one piece that people try to accomplish out of order, putting it first because it seems more interesting or gives them an excuse to shop for all of those captivating organizing supplies. But then they end up with SLES, which is just silly.

When that last box for charity or the local free shredding day has made its way out the door, you can finally relax and look at the space left for creating a system for the stuff you really need to keep. This is the part where you get to be creative. Think about how often you need the item, whether you're short or tall—remember Patrick, from Chapter 4? Can you reach your most-accessed tools at the top of the garage shelving if you're five-two? Consider whether you need visual clues like color-coding or big labels to keep things in place. In my opinion, labels are a must for containers. Not because you don't know what the items are just by looking, but because a label encourages you to keep the items in the same spot all the time. In fact, I almost added "Label" as part of the acronym, but LESSL was also silly.

Think back again to what you learned about yourself in the first part of the project. Are you really going to keep your spices alphabetized all the time, or is that just something you read about in a magazine? What are you realistically willing and able to maintain? Will cardboard boxes do the trick for long-term storage, or should you invest in some sturdier bins? Clutter alert: Don't shop for organizational items until you've completed your sorting, measured your spaces, and checked to see what you already have. Buying ahead often results in buying the wrong things and wasting time and money. Think about your own version of balanced organization—see the definition in Introduction. Are you reaching your orderly Goldilocks zone?

Let's return to the desk drawer example. If you suspect having a divided drawer organizer tray, or several smaller individual ones, would help cut down on the chaos, take a little time to research what's out there. Do not walk into an office supply store or the organizing supplies aisle without an idea of what you want, and do not shop without a list. Get a friend to help you narrow your choices down, if needed. Don't forget to measure the drawer!

You can get creative in the system stage. You don't like files? Don't use them. Some people actually do really well with stacks. Don't like folding T-shirts? Hang them up.

If the system is set up correctly for *you*, you'll know quickly. You won't have to think too terribly hard to get it to work. You may have to try out more than one system to find the best solution, and that's OK. I revise my systems often, because with raising kids and running a business, things change a lot. Organizing is a morphing, elastic, continual process, not a final destination. It is also not a simple, quick-fix kind of thing. It didn't take an hour for your pantry to start overflowing, so why would you think getting and keeping it organized would only take an hour? Please don't get discouraged by those "10 Quick Ways to Get Rid of Clutter Forever!" articles you see, or even by this chapter if it doesn't take at first. Remember Chapter 8? Experiment.

That brings up a significant and touchy point: How long does this whole LESS thing take? It's difficult to say, but what I usually suggest is to imagine how long you think it might take, and double that. If you planned to set aside one day for the garage, make it two. If you finish early, excellent! Enjoy the space you've just created. If you have absolutely no clue how to estimate, start with something small like a shelf or a drawer and time yourself.

LESS works in terms of time, too. You can take your calendar and to-do lists out and walk through everything similar to the way you would handle a closet. Learn what patterns you have in making commitments: Why are you signing up to bring two dishes to the potluck when everyone else brings one? What tasks or commitments don't fit anymore? Which ones do you have to keep, like running the carpool? Which ones do you have a choice about, like signing up to plan the office party? Evaluate and sort your tasks into categories like work, school, volunteering, and social.

You might ask, "What about that rule that says to touch each item only once? We are touching things once to make the decision, once to sort, once to pitch or put." That's true, but it's the way this particular system works. What about that one-in-one-out rule? Or the one that says if you haven't worn it in six months, donate it? Those are solid ideas, too. Have they worked? If LESS is not resonating, I won't be offended. Remember, from the start of this book I've wanted you to discover what *your* organizing balance is. Not what someone else tells you it is. I'm just riffing those variations on a theme here.

But all that said, what would using LESS be like in your garage? Your office? Your car? Your computer? What would it be like to create some organizing balance in those areas?

Now back to your regularly scheduled organizing stories.

CHAPTER 10

It's Still Big and Still Scary

The Story: Melissa

Melissa marched into her laundry room, a woman on a mission. She was lucky, or perhaps not, that the room was large. In addition to the washer and dryer area it had several cabinets on the wall for storage. There was a built-in hanging rod, ironing board, and a tall nook, ideal for things like the vacuum or some mops and brooms. When the house was built, the contractor was thoughtful enough to put a folding counter all across one wall, just below a south-facing window. The room was so much more than the place to wash clothes, too—it was the family nerve center. It was right next to the most-used in and out traffic lane of their home, so it was the logical place for shoes to be kicked off, mail to be opened and sorted, and the wall calendar/white board to hang.

Despite the ample space and well-planned design, there was stuff absolutely everywhere. Plenty of room meant plenty of clutter for this family. Every available inch of surface area was covered, sometimes in layers that could be made out like the cross section of an archeological dig site. The extra, gigantic containers of detergent, refugees from a big box store sale, never seemed to make it from the floor into the cabinet, and if they did, Melissa forgot they existed and bought more. She looked at the mounds of clothing, unsure as usual what was clean and what still needed to be run through a cycle. There were also other things mixed into the piles—school notebooks, gift bags, board game pieces, pet toys. A wall shelf had fallen from the weight of children's backpacks and was never repaired. The room was the family space where nebulous things without homes, like already-graded school science projects and birthday party favor bags, came to languish and die.

Melissa had seen this movie before, the one that usually had an unsatisfying, unresolved ending left up to the audience's imagination. A few months before, she had attacked the room with a vengeance. When she read an inspirational book on decluttering, she dutifully tried everything that was recommended in terms of purging, setting up designated spots for similar items, labeling those spots, and making herself a schedule for keeping up with the loads. A chart was created and posted on the white board for the kids to pitch in, and corresponding rewards determined. Baskets labeled "Clean" and "Dirty" for each family member were procured and lined up in a neat row underneath the folding counter. The cleaning supplies and pet toys were arranged in the cabinets where they belonged, peacefully contained by category in labeled bins.

It was fabulous, and it looked great, and it made her so happy to finally have the room under control. All done! What had been so tough about organizing all of it? It really hadn't been so hard. Melissa had the highest of hopes at the time, the best of intentions—but most of us are familiar with where the best of intentions can lead.

Within about two weeks, things started to slip a little. School let out for a few snow days, and her four children not only added extra laundry, from the tons of layers required for snowball fights and sledding, but also got off their chore schedule. This one small shift seemed to create its own snowball effect, because Melissa felt so disheartened seeing stuff beginning to pile up again that she figured there was really no point in trying to keep up. Within two months of the original purge, random items were once again dumped in the room, everyone was wearing mismatched socks, and she couldn't find simple things like the 9V batteries—naturally—when the smoke alarm started beeping at two in the morning. Still, the door could be shut, so maybe she should just close it and leave it alone. Deep down, she was afraid to try again.

After scrounging through one of the drawers in an unsuccessful search for lip balm, Melissa decided to take another look around that morning. She called yet another family meeting with her husband, kids, and mother-in-law (who lived with them) to get some buy-in and insight for getting back on track. Heads nodded eagerly, because really, they *all* wanted to be able to find clean jeans and underwear easily. What was hard about keeping this particular spot under control? The weirdest part about the situation was that the laundry room was the only room in the house that stayed consistently cluttered. Sure, they could all be a little messy, but this room was the true stuck spot. After some lengthy conversation on delicate cycles, wasted dryer sheets, and the pros and cons of pinning matching socks together, some interesting things opened up.

Through their discussion, Melissa came to realize something: She despised dealing with laundry. She had never even done her own laundry until she went away to college, and mistakes were made. White shirts turned pink, hand wash sweaters were shrunk, and forgotten loads were dumped unceremoniously on the dorm basement floor. When she returned home for visits in between semesters, she was frequently chastised by her perfectionist mother for things like using the wrong temperature, or forgetting to pull the load out as soon as the dryer stopped. She never quite recovered from the feelings of ineptitude and resentment. These feelings, in turn, made her realize that she didn't want her own kids in the same situation. It was why, as soon as they were old enough to shove a load in and push the buttons, she had them doing their own laundry. She had to admit that this training was a good thing—even if they made mistakes, at least they could own them and learn from them.

But when it came to her own stuff, or things like kitchen towels or sheets, Melissa still had very little motivation. She became aware that just looking into the laundry room could be unsettling and irritating, regardless of its degree of order or disarray. More often than not, she would hurriedly run a small load through with just the things she needed right away. She rarely tracked when the kids did or didn't handle their stuff. A backlog would begin, and even the things she had managed to get washed and dried she resisted folding and putting away. This process occurred mindlessly. Paradoxically, as she put things off herself, she would at the same time complain about everyone else's role in the mess. Sensing her stress levels rising, her husband would offer to pitch in and do the loads with her, but sometimes that just made her feel worse, and she became angry and indignant. He was pretty good at laundry, damn it. She thought she *should* be able to handle it all on her own, and instead of being grateful, his ability made her uncomfortable.

After the meeting, and an opportunity to talk about her frustration, Melissa felt a little lighter. The family picked themselves up, dusted themselves off, and discussed starting all over again. There was nothing wrong with the system they had originally put into place. In fact, it made perfect sense, so there was no need to reinvent the wheel. Melissa still found laundry distasteful, but somehow, recognizing why, she gave herself a bit of grace to work with. Perhaps accepting a little more help wouldn't be such a bad idea. Maybe opening up to her discomfort could open up a way to regroup and get back on track. Melissa picked up a basket of towels, and asked if anyone thought they could do a better job with them. Her oldest son's hand shot up, and she happily handed it all over.

The Subplot: I'm No Fun at All

> Give a man a fish and feed him for a day. Teach a man to fish and feed him for a lifetime. Teach a man to cycle and he will realize fishing is stupid and boring.
>
> —Desmond Tutu

I was in the thick of training for this ride. I committed to the metric century, sixty-two miles. I was still getting used to saying the commitment out loud, and I still didn't say it to anyone other than Jeff and KJ. I'd been following a training plan that I found online, only focusing on the length of time I rode rather than the distance or speed. I also tried a little eight-mile family ride a couple of months earlier, the first time I had ridden with other cyclists—who were, mostly, riding the much longer distance option. I managed to get through it pretty easily. Doing almost eight times that distance should be a cakewalk, no?

I took a significant spill on Flo in the early spring of 2018, hitting a patch of mud just the wrong way, falling on my right shoulder and hip. Strangely, even though I experienced the sort of surreal, almost slow-motion feeling of the fall—and yikes, it hurt—I didn't hesitate to get back on and proceed, for that day anyway. To my disgust, I had to take a little break to get the shoulder at least to the point where the pain didn't keep me awake at night. Months later, I paid the price of delaying treatment with ten weeks of physical therapy and several rounds of trigger-point dry needling. I do not recommend ignoring health in the pursuit of your Big Scary Goal.

The online program I started following prescribed three days a week of riding, and I occasionally added in a fourth day for good measure. I cross-trained at least one other day a week. I hydrated like a fish. One Sunday, Jeff and I headed out for the scariest thing I had attempted thus far: thirty miles all on city streets, no greenway, out with the cars and trucks and motorcycles and gravel on the road and potholes and steep hills and everything that still made me feel frightened and inadequate. We rode pretty much from one end of town to the other and back, and perhaps more from mounting frustration and paralyzing fear than a lack of strength, my legs gave out at around twenty-seven miles. I did not have fun on this ride. My arms, neck, and my new trick shoulder were all killing me from the tension I held in throughout the whole soul-sucking experience.

What exactly was I getting from all of this self-inflicted torture? I wasn't sure I was learning a damn thing. All I knew was that it felt terrible, and I didn't feel like I was any good at riding the bike at all. I felt I was making zero progress—we'll set aside the fact that a year prior I couldn't even get out of a parking lot. I still seemed to have issues with basic things like, you know, braking and stopping. I couldn't reliably take a hand off the handlebars yet. I knew that if I hadn't had someone else with me to look behind and check traffic, I wouldn't even have been able to make a left turn. Should it be this difficult? Why was it so pitifully hard for me, and why couldn't I just get over it? I seriously should have been ready. In addition to riding, I'd been reading books and articles, and even watching some videos KJ shared with me. I was trying so hard. I decided that morning that it wasn't fun to ride anymore. I couldn't do it. I had come back around to hating and fearing the process, just like every other time I tried something physical before. Deep down, I still harbored resentment that I hadn't been given much of a chance with it as a kid.

But we still planned a ride for the following week. I don't know what compelled me to try again, other than I had already paid the registration fee for the event, and Jeff asked if we were heading out for the customary longer weekend ride. Resigned to mediocrity and discomfort, I allowed myself to set out on a familiar route that wouldn't tax my wounded pride too much. Instead of trying so hard, I would try so easy and give in to the fact that I was a wimp. You may have noted in the previous paragraphs that I don't give myself much of a break when I don't meet the expectations I have for myself. Unlike Nicole who figured it out in Chapter 8, self-compassion is also an uncomfortable, scary goal for me. It's funny, because I would never talk to a client the way I talk to myself. Can you imagine if I told someone who was frustrated with backsliding that they were making zero progress, or called them a wimp? As I mentioned in that chapter, the self-compassion piece is something I continue to work on. I encourage you to as well.

I parted company with Jeff after the first few miles so he could complete something faster and longer, and some time passed. I was completely by myself when the voice on my fitness tracker announced, "thirty miles," in her robotic, flat voice, although I swear I could detect the smallest bit of approval in her declaration. Wait a second, what was that? You said, thirty miles, yes? Not thirty minutes? Or maybe it was *thirteen* miles? Thirty and thirteen do kind of sound alike, so I stopped and checked the app.

There it was on the screen: 30 MILES. Some of it on streets, some of it on the bike path, but thirty whole miles in total. This bizarre, completely unfamiliar feeling bubbled up out of nowhere in me, and I smiled. I got back on and continued. I wasn't tired. Pretty soon, I was back on a greenway path, dodging toddlers on scooters and elegant ladies in saris, and I'm sure more than a few people thought I was nuts, but I started laughing. Me—I went thirty miles on a bike.

You who have balanced on two wheels without a thought for your whole lives have no idea what a miracle you are. You have no clue how awkward starting, stopping, pedaling, turning, standing, signaling, climbing, or coasting can feel to someone without your sense of natural athletic coordination and balance. Sometimes,

I confess, you piss me off. This whole process had been a complete slog for me, start to not-yet-finished. The most difficult thing to manage had been between my ears. It still is. Sure, it was intimidating most days to actually get on an actual bike and travel actual distances. But the way I thought right before I hopped on was the real thing I hadn't mastered.

The difference between the two rides came down to my expectations. I put a lot of pressure on myself for the former, and almost zero for the latter. Perfectionism and stress versus let's just see what happens. It's like I gave in to my shortcomings, but without actually giving *up*. It came to me in that moment on the ride that I might really be able to do what I set out to do. I didn't anticipate that it would be smooth, fearless sailing, but as far as the endurance to take it to the end went, I thought I might just have it. The crack of hope was widening.

Scribble:

- When and how have you been tough on yourself in this process?
- What is the difference between giving in to a setback and acknowledging it?
- What makes it worth it to try again?

CHAPTER 11

The Rest of the Story

> The bicycle, the bicycle surely, should always be the vehicle of novelists and poets.
>
> —Christopher Morley

I am clearly neither a novelist nor a poet, but perhaps we can make an exception for an aspiring pseudo-autobiographer here. I'm flipping the stories for this last one, because as we began with organizing I think it's only right and proper that we end with it. Or maybe I'm just excited to share the results of my Big Scary Goal journey, even though there were some surprises.

To ride or not to ride. I still hadn't mentioned this goal to many other people, so I didn't have a lot of opinions to collect. I am not one of those people who shouts their aspirations out to the world ahead of time for accountability. I tend to keep my cards close to the vest. I did take a chance and related my idea and scattershot progress with someone I knew was really into bike riding. She politely expressed her skepticism about my ability to complete the whole thing. "Wouldn't you rather finish strong?" she said. "Ride the short distance this time. You can always do a metric century later." One part of me thought she had a point. Another part of me got defensive and irritated. Who was she to tell me what I could or couldn't do? She meant no harm, but that was the last of my sharing.

The week of the event, I debated back and forth with Jeff and KJ about dropping back to the thirty-three-mile ride. I'm sure I drove them a little crazy with my ruminating. How was I going to go from a longest ride of thirty-eight miles to almost double that? Talking about it was making it all worse, so I decided to use a little imagination to visualize the results either way. Maybe if I could feel some possible conclusions out, I could settle my indecision. Indecision was not something I'd ever had many issues with before this event, so not only was it uncomfortable to ponder outcomes, but doubly uncomfortable to admit I was having trouble choosing.

When I pictured riding thirty-three miles, I knew I could do it pretty painlessly. I thought I might even pick up my pace and satisfy myself that it was more than most people would do on an early, summery Saturday morning. I could, as my friend suggested, even choose a different metric century to complete later in the future, but I wondered if I would feel sad that I hadn't tried to go further on that day. Would I just be kicking the Big Scary Goal down the road?

On the other hand, every time I imagined finishing sixty-two, I saw myself wobbling slowly across a finish line, throwing up, falling off of the bike in sheer exhaustion, and being picked up and carted away by alarmed event volunteers. But I could say I finished.

Ultimately, I concluded that no matter how awful and embarrassing the ending, I wanted to finish what I started. So, smart or not, the sixty-two it was. The night before, I was all kinds of jittery nervous. I had no idea what to expect. Had I hydrated enough? Eaten enough? Would I be able to stop safely if a delinquent squirrel ran across my path? Would I panic when eighteen-wheelers barreled past me? What about when I came to a train crossing? If I couldn't finish, and the support and gear (SAG) folks had to come rescue me, would I still have gained anything or gotten any information that I could use to help someone else? Or would I just confirm to myself, once again, that I'm not cut out to do something like this ride? I did not sleep well.

Cutting to the chase, none of my extreme fantasies came to be. The weather cooperated in a big way for us that morning, and despite the heat, we had a nice cloud cover with a few sprinkles of rain here and there. The route was almost totally flat, with just one long hill towards the end. I had two supporters, KJ and one of her friends, with me for moral support and possible disaster rescue. And Jeff was riding as well, although at a speedier, more Jeff-like pace. After the first ten miles or so, I started getting the impression that it wasn't going to be too bad, because I actually felt—dare I say it—strong. Cars were not unnerving me so much. I stopped smoothly at the first water station and had no reluctance to hop back on and continue. I could even look around at the scenic farmland setting and enjoy it, and engage in some silly conversation with my partners in crime. I knew by mile twenty-five that it was going to happen, and it did. I went the whole sixty-two. Not fast, not flashy, and certainly not the way other riders did it, but I completed it. I didn't throw up. And what do you know . . . I wasn't even the last one.

Afterwards there was great rejoicing in Saraland and a celebratory meal. I returned home feeling a combination of amazement and semi-exhaustion, but nothing close to what I had steeled myself for. My tracker indicated I had burned about 1,400 calories, and I was barely even sore the next day.

Once it was all said and done, within the next 24 hours, I quickly spiraled down from my euphoria. I understand that this post-accomplishment letdown is a typical reaction, but I had foolishly thought I would be so aware and realistic with myself that I could control it. I was wrong. I was startled that my deflation occurred so fast. Sure, I finished, but finishing didn't make me any more naturally athletic than I'd ever been. It didn't change my innate ability. I went from amazed to puzzled to bummed.

OK, Sara, so what *did* it do? For starters, it changed my perception of what I could accomplish without much inborn athletic talent. It showed me what fear might or might not affect. It showed me I could be a little more persistent, less willing to hide and accept mediocrity or to give up. It made me quite a bit more fit and definitely pleased with myself for tackling something tough. The whole event was even entertaining and amusing, which was certainly not something I had considered a possibility. I was totally down for several hours of abject misery.

I learned that there is usually a way to figure out how to conquer a Big Scary Goal, if you want it badly enough and are willing to test out many different ways of approaching it. There was no luck, and certainly not much in the way of skill, in my riding the sixty-two miles, except for maybe the happy weather conditions. I worked for those miles, and as you have read, sometimes it felt absolutely impossible and unattainable. The whole thing, start to finish, took almost two years. More than once, I had decided that the entire project was probably not going to come to fruition. I was simultaneously dealing with family and career. God knows that takes up a lot of time, particularly when families are growing and changing. From the time I started this dream until I finished, we had three close deaths in the family and several others slightly more distant, a move, a job change, and kids slowly morphing into semi-adult, sentient beings.

But I also recognized, with some sadness, that there's no way I can completely experience how my clients feel when they can't find their balance. I can't feel their years of frustration and discomfort; I can only feel mine. I can't feel what it's like to let a stranger into a disorganized space that only I am responsible for, because I've never done anything like that. I can only feel what it's like to demonstrate and work through my own lack of ability, discomfort, and fear. I'm not entirely sure they connect. Getting over my fears was probably made much easier, too, by the fact that I had resources available to me that supported the goal. Not everyone has the same resources.

This realization had me discouraged. I was supposed to figure some things out with this little experiment, so I could be some sort of enlightened organizer and passable cyclist. I suddenly felt like I had been incredibly presumptuous. Getting over a fear of riding a bike doesn't really equate in terms of overcoming challenges that are required in order for us to function in this world of schedules, deadlines, and too many choices. Being able to ride a bike is not a necessary skill. You can live a whole, functional, successful life and never learn how to balance on two wheels.

But when I feel a little ridiculous for pinning so much on this ride, I circle it back to people who feel ridiculous for somehow not being able to activate and maintain a better organizing path for themselves. It should be "as easy as riding a bike," right? Reaching out for help, or the concept of having to learn or relearn organization (something that is supposed to be a standard, everyday affair) any time after reaching adulthood seems so mundane, an idea frequently reinforced by friends, family, and our culture. The judgment compounds the discomfort. Whether the reasons are internal or external or both, people struggle with managing stuff, time, and tasks, and they go searching for how to find balance.

So it's not so much that I became coordinated and fast and supremely confident—because I wasn't, and I'm still not. I suppose what has changed is that I now know that none of that matters. I can be uncoordinated, slow, awkward, *still* accomplish the goal, and have fun doing it. I have additional confirmation now that clients without innate organizing skill can overcome sticky challenges too, because I've witnessed it. What usually stands in the way, I think, is the misunderstanding that it all has to occur or look or come about in a specific, prescribed method—and that it can happen quickly and permanently, without ever having to shift or adjust.

What's different when I work with clients now? I now know, without a shadow of a doubt, that big change can happen for anyone. I think I wished and hoped and suspected that it was possible before, but now when I encourage someone in their organizing journey I have a different sort of confidence. I know that by letting go of external messages, embracing their fear and discomfort, and asking for help when they need it, that they can achieve unexpected results and stay consistent. I also developed a much deeper appreciation for my own organizing ability—I will never take it for granted.

I was also sure I wanted to keep riding, but I now had a new fear to contend with: What if I didn't? Like Rachel mused in Chapter 2, what if I just settled back into an old routine that was more comfortable? As I finished up that chapter, a cold, mid-February rainstorm was pouring outside, and riding that century seemed a long-distant feat. What if I got this book written, with everything all tied up happily and neatly, and I just went back to being Sara, the unathletic woman who is terrified to ride a bike?

I took Flo out one early spring day just to ride for fun. I was happily anticipating that just heading out on one of my regular routes with no agenda, no particular goal in mind, would be the easy-peasy experience I would finally get to have. You know, like everyone else. But when I pulled her down from the bike rack and hopped on, that old discomfort and anxiety came right back. I wobbled a little on the start, and the hill I was staring down suddenly looked too steep, and that stabbing feeling popped up in my solar plexus. My breathing was shallow, I was a little shaky, and I gripped those handlebars like I was hanging on to the edge of a cliff. I stopped and got off. Shook myself. Got back on. What the actual heck? I hadn't felt that level of fear in weeks, maybe even months. Where was it coming from?

I didn't, and still don't know, but I do know that I accepted my momentary panic. I pushed off and went down the hill anyway. Maybe subconsciously the memory of my brother's accident, or my lack of natural skill, or my parents' paranoia will always be floating around in my soul. Sometimes, when I ride now, I'm relaxed; sometimes I'm not. I do know this:

It's the only form of activity that I want to go back to the minute I hop off. It's the only challenging physical activity that I'm sad to stop when I finish.

On to one hundred miles now? Or maybe . . . something else?

©Sara Skillen

Yes. Because you know, I never really learned how to do this very well, either.

The Last Story: Amelia

> The only difference between a mob and a trained army is organization.
>
> —Calvin Coolidge

Amelia is nearing the end of her Big Scary Goal journey: organizing and simplifying her whole house—really, her whole life. For the better part of eighteen months, she has systematically worked through things like planning challenges, purging obsolete paperwork in her home office, cutting back on her impulse buying, and categorizing all of her old hard copy photos. She's emptied and reset every closet and drawer in the house and tackled the boxes from her own and her husband and son's childhoods with a vengeance. Amelia is now a woman with a consistent and determined focus on finding the right-for-her organizing balance. Let's see how she got there.

She hired a professional organizer to get her jump-started in the beginning, but she stopped that particular support after they got her scariest, most challenging area, the attic storage space, completed. The organizer did a great job of transferring some basic organizing skills to her, giving her a customized system to follow and helping her to shop in her own home for organizing supplies and resources—there was, fortunately, plenty to choose from.

Amelia sometimes still heard her organizer's voice in her head repeating clutter-control mantras such as:

- "Does this item make you more successful?"
- "When was the last time you used it?"
- "Will you think of it again two weeks from now?"
- "Did you make your list?"
- "Do you *need* another notebook? Another app? Another file system?"
- "Where does your brain tell you to look for this item?"
- "How will you feel when you can see the top of the desk?"

After conquering the first goal, she used a combination of an inspiring organizing book and a tennis club friend to support the process and keep her invested. She traded her friend some bookkeeping help in exchange for encouraging her through getting rid of old clothes and toys. When she completed a space, she rewarded herself with a new experience, like checking out a local attraction with friends or trying a new coffee shop. Despite a few dry spells (losing interest is normal) and a little backsliding (she has a bit of a weakness for independent bookstores), she recovered each time and got back into her groove. It has taken a long time in the scheme of things, but taking that time was so much better than the alternative of never even starting.

Sometimes her progress completely stalled, like when she left for a weeklong girls' vacation to the beach. When she returned home, tanned and relaxed, she was deflated to learn her husband and teenaged son had, shall we say, undone a few of the things she had gotten into place. They weren't purposely trying to be difficult, they just didn't always recognize her efforts or totally embrace the idea that it's just as easy to put something away as it is to drop it on the floor.

She was hugely discouraged to open the hall closet door and find everything—from hockey gear to water bottles to excess school supplies—tumbling out. The kitchen drawers were jumbled and out of whack too. She even felt some doubt and fear about whether or not these occurrences were a sign of the beginning of the end. The end of those organizing life battles that were so carefully fought and won. Maybe there wasn't even any point in the whole exercise if others were just going to keep goofing everything up for her. But after some pointed discussions and time pitching in together, the closet and drawers went back to normal.

So here she is now, continuing to give herself some grace, accepting the backsliding without criticizing herself: Amelia still sometimes falls off her metaphorical bike, takes a moment to nurse the hurt, shakes the dust off, and hops back on. She regains her balance, uncertainty or no, and continues. Her yardstick for organizing success is not connected to what she sees in magazines or online, or on TV, or even friends' or family members' homes. Rather, it's tied to how she feels in her surroundings, whether or not she can find things easily, and whether she functions with so little stress that she can think about the fun and productive things she wants to do with her life.

She still doesn't consider herself naturally organized, but she also no longer cares about having that label. She cares that at the end of the day there is some degree of order, that the most important balls have been caught. If she walks into her home and senses peace, it's all good. If she looks around and feels antsy, it's time to do a little work.

Taking the steps to stay on top of the stuff and tasks has become comfortable enough that now it *is* on the same level as brushing her teeth or tying her shoes. It's automatic to the point that she can think about other things while she's doing it, if she wants to. Or she can make it a more mindful, meditative, even comforting sort of activity. Organization isn't a one-time event, but a way of moving through her full and often complicated world. Her organization doesn't look like anyone else's, nor should it. It looks like her life, and she appreciates it.

Where do *you* go from here? Having tackled a Big Scary Goal, do you follow up and clear out a basement, or the home office, or your running to-do list? Do you want to commit to using a calendar daily, or opening and sorting your mail, or some other regular habit that bit by bit will get you closer to a calmer existence? It is more fun, or perhaps allows more fun, to have a comfortable level of organization and productivity in your life, once you become accustomed to it.

Your Big Scary Goal might be way tougher than mine, or it might be easier. I don't think that matters now, because it's yours to balance. It may feel silly and embarrassing to admit to anyone. That's fine—you can keep it to yourself at first. You might decide to start, then stop, and then start again. You may want help, or you might want to fly solo. The goal may keep you up at night with doubts. It might frustrate you when you recognize how uncomfortable your surroundings are and then admit how uncomfortable it is to change them. Allow yourself that discomfort, invite yourself to make some moves and shifts, and even give up completely. Then come back again, learn more, and take it all further than you ever expected.

Acknowledgements

It is another cliché that it takes many people to create a book, and when I think back over this process from the beginning, I know I have a monumental task ahead to include everyone here. But here goes.

First, I am eternally grateful to Terry Huff for his guidance, feedback, encouragement, and gentle insistence on keeping me "out on the ledge" while I wrote. In many ways, writing this book has been one giant ball of discomfort, and it would never have gotten out of my head and computer without his support and wisdom.

To KJ Garner, who is a physical and mental representation of balance in many ways, I am forever indebted. Not only did she patiently teach, allow me to write about the experience, and stick with me through a long ride (when I know she could have finished much faster), she gave me the gift of being able to laugh on a bike again. I'm thankful to Janet Tuck, who knows why I had to write. Many thanks to Mary Rice for her fantastic photographs, and to Bridget Filipovic who bravely let me use her closet as the example in Chapter 1. Many thanks also to

Susan Lindsey and Sarah Haywood for their editing support. I learned a great deal in that process. To Kelly Santaguida at Gatekeeper Press, I so appreciate your support, responsiveness, and patience.

To Laura Huff Hileman, Geralin Thomas, Cindy Chafin, Larry Price, Karen Shayne, Joyce Johnson, and anyone else who ever said, "Hey, you ought to write a book," now you know that I was actually listening. Thanks to Susan Lieber, Caroline Hensley, and Francesca Maas, who gave late-in-the-game, super valuable feedback. I'm deeply grateful to my clients who also encouraged me, listened and experimented as I tried out some of my ideas on making friends with discomfort, and who promised to finish reading an entire book on organization—you know who you are!

To our children, Cameron and Wyatt, who had to walk past my closed office door more often than they might have liked, thank you for being the amazing humans you are, just as you are. It's such an honor and privilege to be your mom. And finally, especially big love and eternal gratitude to Jeff, for being a patient rock, advisor, and cheerleader throughout this lengthy process—and of course, for introducing me to Flo.

Acknowledgements

© Sara S. Skillen

References

IKEA Infographic. "The State of Storage and Organization in U.S. Homes." ©2013.

Wilder, Laura Ingalls. *Little House In The Big Woods.* Trophy Edition. New York, NY: HarperCollins, 1971.

Peterson, Grant. *Just Ride: A Radically Practical Guide To Riding Your Bike.* Kindle Edition. New York, NY: Workman Publishing Company, Inc., 2012.

Rohr, Richard. "Change As A Catalyst For Transformation." June 30, 2016. https://cac.org/change-catalyst-transformation-2016-06-30/.

O'Donohue, John. *Anam Cara: A Book Of Celtic Wisdom.* Kindle Edition. New York, NY: HarperCollins, 1997.

Other Helpful Books (in no particular order)

The Practicing Mind by Thomas M. Sterner

Embracing Fear: How To Turn What Scares Us Into Our Greatest Gift by Thom Rutledge

The Mindful Path To Self-Compassion by Christopher K. Germer, PhD

www.ingramcontent.com/pod-product-compliance
Lightning Source LLC
LaVergne TN
LVHW011832060526
838200LV00053B/3983